Islamophobia

Islamophobia

An Anthology of Concerns

Edited by Emma Webb

CIVITAS

First Published August 2019

© Civitas 2019
55 Tufton Street
London SW1P 3QL

email: books@civitas.org.uk

ISBN 978-1-906837-98-3

Independence: Civitas: Institute for the Study of Civil
Society is a registered educational charity (No. 1085494)
and a company limited by guarantee (No. 04023541).
Civitas is financed from a variety of private sources to
avoid over-reliance on any single or small group of donors.

All the Institute's publications seek to further its objective
of promoting the advancement of learning. The views
expressed are those of the authors, not of the Institute.

Typeset by Typetechnique

Printed in Great Britain by
4edge Limited, Essex

'This comprehensive anthology of widespread concerns about the danger to free speech and legitimate discussion in the use of the vague catch-all term Islamophobia, is both timely and welcome.

'The report will not only help protect free speech and legitimate criticism, but also help us understand why Muslims and other religious communities are sometimes the target for hate crimes that shame society. Perpetrators of such crimes do not carry out a detailed study of a religion before expressing antipathy. Hatred arises out of ignorance in which small differences can assume frightening and threatening proportions. It can only be removed through greater emphasis on religious and cultural literacy.'

Lord Singh of Wimbledon

'Islamophobia is an otiose word which doesn't deserve definition. Hatred of Muslims is unequivocally reprehensible, as is hatred of any group of people such as gay people or members of a race. Hatred of Islam, on the other hand is easily justified, as is hatred of any other religion or obnoxious ideology. Muslims themselves are the main victims of Islam.'

Professor Richard Dawkins

Acknowledgements

The editor would like to thank Dr David Green, director of Civitas, for his support and colleagues Liam Duffy and Atlanta Neudorf for their assistance in compiling this anthology.

Contents

Authors

Emma Webb is director of the Forum on Integration, Democracy and Extremism (FIDE), a project of Civitas. She was formerly a research fellow at the Centre on Radicalisation and Terrorism (CRT) at the Henry Jackson Society. Her published work focuses on Islamist extremist networks and their abuse of civil society, the education and charitable sectors, and domestic funding. She has been published in *The Times*, the *Telegraph*, *Independent* and *Spectator*, among others and has appeared on international media discussing the risks posed by terrorism and extremism in Europe. Emma holds degrees from the University of Cambridge and King's College London.

Dr Rumy Hasan is senior lecturer at Science Policy Research Unit at the University of Sussex. Since 2005 his work has focused on issues relating to multiculturalism, multifaithism, and social cohesion; and the nexus between religion (especially Islam) identity, and society. He is the author of *Multiculturalism: Some Inconvenient Truths* (2010) and has written extensively on the topic of Islamophobia.

Peter Tatchell is director of the human rights organisation, the Peter Tatchell Foundation. He is a renowned campaigner for equality and democracy. While defending the right of religious people to hold their beliefs, he opposes them using these beliefs to suppress criticism or justify discrimination.

Dr David Green is the chief executive of Civitas, which he founded in 2000. David has written for *The Sunday Times*, *The Times*, *The Sunday Telegraph* and *The Daily Telegraph*, among others, and has appeared on programmes such as Newsnight, Moral Maze, and the Today programme. David was formerly a Labour councillor in Newcastle upon Tyne, a research fellow at the Australian National University in Canberra and directed the Health and Welfare Unit of the Institute for Economic Affairs from 1986-2000. In 2006, David was a member of the Home Secretary's Crime Statistics Review Group.

Professor Paul Cliteur is professor of Jurisprudence at Leiden University in the Netherlands. He is the author and editor of a number of volumes, including *Theoterrorism v Freedom of Speech: From Incident to Precedent (2019) and The Secular Outlook: In Defence of Moral and Political Secularism (2015).*

Tim Dieppe is head of public policy at Christian Concern. Tim holds degrees from the University of Oxford and Westminster Theological College.

Hardeep Singh is a freelance journalist, deputy-director for the Network of Sikh Organisations and Assistant Editor of The Sikh Messenger. He was a leading member of the Libel Reform Campaign, along with science writer Simon Singh and cardiologist Dr Peter Wilmshurst. He has co-authored the forthcoming volume *Racialization, Islamophobia and Mistaken Identity: The Sikh Experience* and wrote a chapter titled 'Religious Libel: are the courts the right place for faith disputes' for *Legal Cases, New Religious Movements and Minority Faith*s. He has written for the the *Telegraph*, *The Spectator*, *The Guardian*, *The Independent*, *IBTimes UK*, *Legal Week*, *The Lawyer*, *Media Lawyer*, *Spiked*, *Quillette*, *New Humanist* and *Index on Censorship*.

Pragna Patel is a founder and director of Southall Black Sisters' advice and advocacy centre. She has been centrally involved in some of SBS' most important cases and campaigns around domestic violence, immigration and religious fundamentalism and has written extensively on race, gender and religion. Southall Black Sisters, a not-for-profit, secular and inclusive organisation, was established in 1979 to meet the needs of Black (Asian and African-Caribbean) and minority women.

Ed Husain is Senior Fellow and Director of Islam, the West and Geopolitics at Civitas. Ed is author *House of Islam: A Global History* (2018) and the bestselling book *The Islamist* (Penguin, 2007). Ed writes and speaks extensively on the geopolitics of the Middle East, international threats from radicalisation and terrorism. He was a senior advisor to former prime minister Tony Blair. He has appeared on CNN, Fox, NPR, BBC, and Al-Jazeera, and writes regularly for publications including the *New York Times*, *Financial Times* and the *Guardian*.

Maryam Namazie is an Iranian-born writer and activist. She is the Spokesperson for Fitnah – Movement for Women's Liberation, One Law for All and the Council of Ex-Muslims of Britain. Namazie is on the International Advisory Board of the Raif Badawi Foundation for Freedom and Euromind; National Secular Society Honorary Associate; Honorary Associate of Rationalist International; Emeritus Member of the Secular Humanist League of Brazil and a Patron of Pink Triangle Trust.

Mohammed Amin MBE was formerly chairman of the Conservative Muslim Forum. He has travelled in life from a village in the Pakistani Punjab to the streets of Manchester,

Clare College Cambridge, and then a partnership in PricewaterhouseCoopers. In retirement he is active in many organisations, and also writes and speaks regularly on Islam, politics and community cohesion.

The National Secular Society campaigns for the separation of religion and state and equal respect for everyone's human rights, so no one is either advantaged or disadvantaged because of their beliefs. The National Secular Society is a non-party-political organisation with members from across the social and political spectrum. Their Honorary Associates include MPs and peers, as well as leading figures from politics, journalism, law and the arts.

David Toube is Director of Policy at the Quilliam Foundation. David was educated at Southampton University and at Brasenose College, Oxford, and is a barrister by training. He taught law at Queen Mary University of London, and then practiced law for 25 years, where he headed the European bank regulatory practice of a prominent international law firm. David has been active in counter-extremism activism and writing for fifteen years, and has written for *The Guardian* and other news outlets. His focus is on far Left, far Right and Islamist extremism, and on extremism, polarisation and conspiracism within political culture.

'Islamophobia is rooted in racism and is a type of racism that targets expressions of Muslimness or perceived Muslimness.'

APPG on British Muslims proposed definition of Islamophobia

Introduction

In November 2018 the All-Party Parliamentary Group (APPG) on British Muslims, chaired by Anna Soubry MP, published its report, *Islamophobia Defined*, to establish a working definition of Islamophobia. Subsequently the definition has been adopted by local councils and political parties, even before the Home Affairs Select Committee have concluded their assessment of the proposed definition, which remains ongoing at the time of writing.

This volume brings together concerns about the APPG definition of Islamophobia from a variety of perspectives. It includes atheist, secularist, religious and academic assessments of why the Islamophobia definition is not only unfit for purpose, but also poses a danger to civil liberties in the United Kingdom, particularly freedom of expression, and journalistic and academic freedom. An open letter signed by over 40 faith leaders and experts can be found in the appendix.

Emma Webb

No convincing case has been made that the current provisions of the law are insufficient to deal with discrimination against or violence towards Muslim individuals (Crime and Disorder Act 1998; Public Order Act 1986).[1] Preventing discrimination against individuals on the basis of their religion, alongside other protected categories, is already enshrined in legislation.

The APPG definition is explicit in its desire to expand the definition into hitherto uncovered areas, but did not make a convincing case for the necessity of a specific definition of Islamophobia. The proposed definition stands in contradiction to the Waddington Amendment (Public Order Act 1986, section 29J) that protects 'discussion, criticism or expressions of antipathy, dislike, ridicule, insult or abuse of particular religions or the beliefs or practices of their adherents, or of any other belief system or the beliefs or practices of its adherents, or proselytising or urging adherents of a different religion or belief system to cease practising their religion or belief system.' The adoption of this definition would have a chilling effect on free expression, criticism of Islam and related ideologies, such as Islamism.

Explored in detail below, additional concerns about the APPG's definition of Islamophobia and its implications are as follows:

---

[1] 'What is a hate crime?' *Metropolitan Police*, available at: https://www.met.police.uk/advice/advice-and-information/hco/hate-crime/what-is-hate-crime/

- The vague, expansive and jargonistic nature of the definition and its confusing conflation of religion and race in employing the term 'cultural racism';

- The lack of parity between the concepts of antisemitism and the APPG's understanding of Islamophobia do not justify the transposition of the IHRA definition in the case of anti-Muslim hatred, which is more limited in scope. A proactive approach that is compatible with a free society, encouraging integration and good community relations, would be more acceptable in countering broader anti-Muslim sentiments that are not appropriate subjects of legislation;

- A lack of due diligence and partiality in the collection and treatment of written and oral evidence by the APPG;

- Negative implications of the definition for freedom of expression and its impact on journalists, researchers and the public;

- Negative ramifications for the efficacy of the integration and counter-extremism policy, and its potential effect on different sectors, such as education.

Current Legal Provision is Sufficient and Appropriate

In agreement with Baroness Falkner (House of Lords debate, 20 December 2018), 'much of the response must come from existing criminal and civil law and guidance, rather than the creation of new criminal definitions and categories'. The APPG report repeatedly insists that the adoption of its definition would be impactful but does not convincingly evidence this claim.

The APPG states that the threshold under current legislation is too low (p. 21) and defines Islamophobia in a way which goes beyond 'what can be captured as criminal acts', including so-called 'micro-aggressions' (p. 32). Is encompassing so many complex problems in a single hold-all, expansive term appropriate in a free society?

'Anti-Muslim hatred' is more narrowly defined and its application is both limited and safer. Anti-Muslim hatred ought to be treated as equal to anti-Christian, anti-Sikh, or anti-Hindu (et cetera) hatred, abuse and discrimination. Setting off down the path of defining '-phobias' for each group in society could represent a counter-productive 'creep towards communal identity politics'.[2] To quote Swiss-Yemeni academic Elham Manea, 'once the state starts to situate rights within the frame of a group rather than within the individual, the likely outcome will be segregation, inequality and discrimination'.[3]

In addition, due to the complex and ambiguous nature of recording hateful motivations behind criminal or discriminatory incidents, the statistics are not straightforward. For example, a 2017 investigation by Hardeep Singh shows that the 1,227 recorded Islamophobic incidents in 2016 included Christians (39), Hindus (19), Atheists (11), Sikhs (4), Greek Orthodox (2), Jews (2) and Catholics (2). Although concerningly high, only 912 of those recorded were actually Muslim. In 86 cases the victim's religion was not known, and 57 had never been contacted.[4] Concerns have also been raised in relation to an apparent

---

[2] John Jenkins, 'Defining Islamophobia: A Policy Exchange Research Note'', *Policy Exchange* https://policyexchange.org.uk/wp-content/uploads/2018/12/Defining-Islamophobia.pdf, p. 9.

[3] Elham Manea, *Women and Shari'a Law* (London, I. B. Taurus, 2016), p. 54.

[4] Lord Morrow (DUP), Religious Intolerance and Prejudice Debate, *House of Lords*, 17 October 2018, available at: https://hansard.parliament.uk/Lords/2018-10-17/debates/FC5A8FC0-FAFF-435B-B9E5-C5DBFB16465D/ReligiousIntoleranceAndPrejudice#contribution-AB62E092-EBE8-41EC-8954-4607D3989C35

increase in crime against Christians[5] and the lack of attention paid to non-Abrahamic faith communities[6] As argued by the Network of Sikh Organisations (NSO) these can be dealt with within the current provisions of the law and do not require any special individual definitions.[7]

Vague and Expansive Definition

The definition proposed by the APPG is vague, expansive and unworkable. It attempts to encompass too many problems, ranging from micro-aggressions to subtle hard-to-identify (or sufficiently evidence) structural biases. The use of the term 'Muslimness' begs the question: who will be the arbiter of this? What about those Muslims who, to echo Baroness Falkner and Counter Extremism Commissioner Sara Khan, are thought by other Muslims to be insufficiently Muslim?[8] 'Cultural racism' – the concept on which the definition draws – is not convincing. The phrase is a conflation, gerrymanders plain meaning, and is unsuitable as a definition.

The use of this questionable concept allows the APPG to draw false parity with antisemitism and therefore emulate the IHRA definition of antisemitism. Antisemitism is a very specific racial concept and is directly equivalent to anti-Jewish hatred, abuse or violence. The need for a separate term is based on the fact that, uniquely among religions,

---

[5] Hardeep Singh, 'Is Britain becoming a Christianophobic Country?', *Spectator*, 7 November 2017, available at: https://blogs.spectator.co.uk/2017/11/is-britain-becoming-a-christianophobic-country/

[6] 'NSO gives evidence on APPG on British Muslims on Islamophobia', *Network of Sikh Organisations*, 6 June 2018, available at: http://nsouk.co.uk/nso-gives-evidence-to-appg-on-british-muslims-on-islamophobia/

[7] ibid.

[8] Sara Khan, 'We are still ignoring victims of anti-Muslim prejudice', *Huffington Post*, 3 December 2018, available at: https://www.huffingtonpost.co.uk/entry/islamophobia-extremism-hate-crime-racism_uk_5c0566e8e4b066b5cfa475a3

the Jewish community has historically (and as a result of doctrine) been ascribed a dimension of 'peoplehood' or ethnicity. Islam explicitly does not have such an element. The concept of antisemitism does not extend to include criticisms of Judaism (even if they are instrumentalised with malign intent) or of Jewishness. Whereas the proposed Islamophobia definition has been explicitly broadened beyond the plain meaning of 'anti-Muslim hatred'.

Lack of Due Diligence and Partiality in the Treatment of Evidence

Concerns have rightly been publicly raised about the strong influence of certain organisations over the conclusions of the APPG report[9] and that the report heavily draws on, but does not engage critically with, evidence submitted by academics of a similar stripe. I agree with these observations but will not rehearse them in detail.[10] This is compounded by the dismissive and incomplete treatment of dissenting sources. Evidence submitted by the National Secular Society, Dr Rumy Hasan, Southall Black Sisters and Lord Singh of Wimbledon, were selectively cited only as a means to rebuff them (e.g. pp. 37-38).[11] The impartiality of the APPG is brought into question when following Lord Singh's Oral

---

[9] Baroness Falkner of Margravine, 'Islamophobia', House of Lords Hansard, 20 December 2018, available at: https://hansard.parliament.uk/lords/2018-12-20/ debates/2F954D45-1962-4256-A492-22EBF6AEF8F0/Islamophobia; Jenkins, John., 'Defining Islamophobia: A Policy Exchange Research Note'', Policy Exchange

[10] Baroness Falkner of Margravine, 'Islamophobia', *House of Lords Hansard*, 20 December 2018; John Jenkins, 'Defining Islamophobia: A Policy Exchange Research Note'', *Policy Exchange* https://policyexchange.org.uk/wp-content/ uploads/2018/12/Defining-Islamophobia.pdf;

[11] e.g. 'NSO gives evidence on APPG on British Muslims on Islamophobia', *Network of Sikh Organisations*, 6 June 2018.

Evidence, Baroness Warsi stated 'I disagree with everything you've said Lord Singh'.[12]

The Southall Black Sisters' evidence was treated exceptionally critically: 'The argument', the report says 'appears highly misguided' (p. 42, cf. 43). Dr Rumy Hasan's evidence was either misunderstood or misread in such a way that it was undermined. When Dr Hasan stated that 'Islam... is an ideology like any other religious or non-religious ideology', the report comments that this 'sits awkwardly within the debate' because Dr Hasan 'defines Islam (a religion) as an ideology...while describing Christianity and Judaism, appropriately, as religions'. The plain meaning of Dr Hasan's evidence is that he defines all religions as ideologies, and he is not, as the APPG seem to suggest, making an exception of Islam.

Additionally, positive news stories about Muslims in Britain were overlooked and a long list of unsubstantiated statements go without critical engagement, creating a potentially distorted but bleak picture of Muslim life in the UK.[13] Despite claims to have widely consulted the Muslim community, no Ahmadiyya groups appear to have contributed – a Muslim community much maligned by Islamists.

Negative Impact on Freedom of Speech

I agree with the National Secular Society that the APPG definition risks undermining free speech by conflating criticism of Islam with anti-Muslim bigotry and that, as the Society stated, the government 'must not treat the civil

---

7

liberties of British citizens as an afterthought in its efforts to tackle anti-Muslim prejudice'

The report (e.g. p. 11) and subsequent comments by Baroness Warsi (Debate, House of Lords, 20 December 2018) insist that free speech is respected by the definition. However, the content undermines these assurances, giving the impression of gaslighting. The way in which the Baroness employs the term in that debate may be taken as illustrative of how it could be used to ill effect.

The Baroness stated that 'It only serves to demonstrate the necessity of the definition itself—to call out those anti-Semites or Islamophobes who poison our politics and society. In the case of one such critic, for example, *Sunday Times* journalist Andrew Gilligan.' Andrew Gilligan's work legitimately investigates Islamist activity. The Baroness suggests that Gilligan's reasonable objections are nothing but 'self-preservation'. Does this imply that should the definition be made statutory, he would be unable to continue his work as before? This is valuable work that should not be restricted.

I am extremely concerned by the APPG's notion of 'reasonable' (p. 30) or 'legitimate' (p. 35) and their lack of serious engagement with relevant free speech concerns (e.g. 'Giving up the term islamophobia – and with it the possibility of creating legal instruments to tackle it – simply because of the perceived risk that it may limit free speech would be highly misguided', p. 35).

The circular logic of dismissing free speech concerns by attributing to them 'Islamophobic' motives is problematic. The report states 'the recourse to the notion of free speech and a supposed right to criticise Islam results in nothing more than another subtle form of anti-Muslim racism, whereby criticism humiliates, marginalises, and stigmatises Muslims', and gives the example of grooming gangs. The report states that calling Mohammed a paedophile does not have the victim as the subject of the statement, but that its intention is to harm and it is 'not rooted in any meaningful theological debate'. (p. 35).

This is possible because one of the '5 tests' found to be useful by the APPG in discriminating between legitimate and illegitimate criticism of Islam is whether the comment was made for sincere or ulterior motives (p. 36). Who would be the arbiter in such cases? In a free society, there can be no arbitration of which criticisms of any given religion or ideology are legitimate, regardless of perceived motive, level of education or quality of debate.

The broadening of the definition of Islamophobia to ambiguously include 'illegitimate' criticisms of Islam is highly worrying (cf. pp., 9, 23, 24, 27, 30). Not only does the APPG fail to give any examples of what would constitute legitimate criticism, the illustrations it does provide of Islamophobic speech should be permitted in free society. These include: accusing Muslims of entryism into politics, government or other societal institutions; accusing Muslims of being more loyal to the 'Ummah' than their nation of residence; saying Muhammad is a paedophile; and claiming Muslims spread Islam by the sword or subjugate minority groups. Of course, if such claims are libellous all should have recourse to justice through normal routes.

The definition would have a chilling effect on necessary discussion around the Islamist threat to the UK.

Negative Impact on Integration and Counter-Extremism Work

One might ask: what of – feminist or LGBT thinkers/activists who criticise Islamic attitudes to gender and sexuality? – Secular or moderate Muslims who criticise the wearing of the burqa, niqab or hijab? – Journalists or researchers who investigate Islamist entryism, such as in the case of Lutfur Rahman in Tower Hamlets? Two examples serve to show potential negative effects of the definition:

First, Ofsted have expressed concerns relating to community pressure, particularly from conservative religious groups, being exerted on schools. This was made clear in Amanda Spielman's letter to the Public Accounts Committee on 30 November 2018. As was seen with the case of segregation and gender discrimination at one school in Birmingham, 'religious group identity and authority', Spielman said in July 2018, 'are being systematically built up and used to limit individual liberties, such as the right of a girl to enjoy the same freedoms and opportunities as a boy'.[14]

Another example is the case of St Stephen's School in Newham, East London. In September 2017, the school instituted a ban on children under the age of 8 years old from wearing the hijab, not normally worn until after puberty.[15] The headteacher consequently suffered abuse and pressure and eventually reversed the ban. According to an investigation by the *Daily Mail* hundreds of identical emails sent to the headteacher originated with a template authored Mend, who claimed that the reversal was an 'important step towards resolving concerns about structural Islamophobia'.[16] Ofsted were subsequently

---

[14] 'Amanda Spielman's Speech to Policy Exchange Think Tank', *Ofsted*, 9 July 2018, available at: https://www.gov.uk/government/speeches/amanda-spielmans-speech-to-the-policy-exchange-think-tank

[15] 'Extremists who bullied an inspiring primary school headteacher into reversing a ban on hijabs in the classrooms', *Daily Mail*, 2 February 2018, available at: https://www.dailymail.co.uk/news/article-5346605/Extremists-bullied-head-hijab-ban-u-turn-exposed.html

[16] ibid.

accused of 'Islamophobia'.[17] Others accused of the same include Dominic Kennedy, for his journalistic reporting on Islamism, as are Muslims working in counter-extremism,[18] such as Sara Khan and Maajid Nawaz.[19]

Second, there is ample evidence of the problems of Islamist abuse of the charitable sector.[20] Baroness Warsi has herself claimed that Muslim charities are unfairly vilified (23 February 2017), while giving a speech at the inaugural Muslim Charities Forum (MCF) Humanitarian Awards.[21] MCF was stripped of government funding in 2015 due to alleged funding links to Hamas and the Muslim Brotherhood.[22]

Would attempts to expose and deal with Islamist abuse of charities be hampered by the accusation of Islamophobia employing the APPG definition, and if so, where would this leave the Charity Commission's policies and its objectives, as well as public trust in the sector?

---

[17] 'Ofsted's Amanda Spielman panders to tabloids in another ideologically driven speech', *Islam 21c*, 13 July 2018, available at: https://www.islam21c.com/politics/ofsteds-amanda-spielman-panders-to-tabloids-in-another-ideologically-driven-speech/

[18] 'The Truth about Dominic Kennedy's Hate', *Mend*, available at: https://mend.org.uk/wp-content/uploads/2017/04/The-Truth-about-Dominic-Kennedys-Hate.pdf

[19] Andrew Gilligan, 'The Danger of the 'Islamophobia' label', *Spectator*, 8 December 2018.

[20] Emma Webb, 'Wolves in Sheep's Clothing: How Islamist extremists exploit the UK charitable sector', *Henry Jackson Society* (2018).

[21] 'Muslim charities have been vilified, says Baroness Warsi', *Third Sector*, 23 February 2018, available at: https://www.thirdsector.co.uk/muslim-charities-vilified-says-baroness-warsi/policy-and-politics/article/1425226

[22] 'Muslim charity stripped of state funding over extremism fears', *Daily Telegraph*, 11 January 2015, available at: https://www.telegraph.co.uk/news/politics/conservative/11337846/Muslim-charity-stripped-of-state-funding-over-extremism-fears.html

Conclusion

I have called upon the Home Affairs Select Committee on Islamophobia to consider the weight of concern expressed in many quarters about the harmful implications of this definition, particularly on freedom of expression and the consequences for those carrying out research, journalistic or academic, into Islamism. I also asked the Committee to question the method for collecting and assessing the evidence submitted to the APPG, the lack of due diligence and potential bias, and its consequences for their conclusions.

Dr Rumy Hasan

Runnymede Trust's Report on Islamophobia, 1997

The decisive factor behind the appellation of 'Islamophobia' was the publication, in 1997, of a report by The Runnymede Trust's 'Commission on British Muslims and Islamophobia' entitled *Islamophobia: a Challenge for Us All*. The raison d'être of the report flows from its definition of Islamophobia (p. 4):

> The term Islamophobia refers to an unfounded hostility towards Islam. It refers also to the practical consequences of such hostility in unfair discrimination against Muslim individuals and communities, and to the exclusion of Muslims from mainstream political and social affairs.

The reason why it is a 'phobia' is because of *unfounded* hostility – which approximates to the more conventional 'irrational fear'. But there can, of course, be a rational basis for a fear or a well-founded hostility, which the report does not allow for. Therefore, its thrust is that any hostility towards Islam and Muslims is deemed unfounded and, therefore, Islamophobic. It is this reasoning that makes the term so problematic and misplaced in grappling with the realities in their multitudinous forms.

The report does, however, make this important admission:

> The term is not, admittedly, ideal. Critics of it consider that its use panders to what they call political correctness, that it stifles legitimate criticism of Islam, and that it demonises and stigmatises anyone who wishes to engage in such criticism.

This caveat was absolutely correct and the Runnymede Trust should have desisted from invoking this loaded term.

Views of British Muslims

An extensive ICM Poll of British Muslims for Channel 4 conducted in 2015 found that:

- A large majority of British Muslims feel a strong sense of belonging to Britain (86%). This is higher than the national average (83%);

- A large majority of British Muslims feel that they are able to practice their religion freely in Britain (94%);

- British Muslims are more likely than the rest of the population to feel that they can influence decisions affecting Britain (33% vs 21%);

- British Muslims are more likely than the rest of the population to feel that their local MP reflects their views (44% vs 41%);

- 88% of British Muslims think that Britain is a good place for Muslims to live.[1]

These findings robustly challenge the view that Muslims in Britain are subject to systematic discrimination and harassment which form the basis for the supposed existence of 'Islamophobia'.

Context

The increase in suspicion, discrimination, and the temporary, sporadic surge in violence and aggression towards some

---

[1] 'C4 survey and documentary reveals What British Muslims Really Think', *Channel 4*, 11 April 2016 https://www.channel4.com/press/news/c4-survey-and-documentary-reveals-what-british-muslims-really-think

Muslims in Britain after the July 7th 2005 bombings in London has to be seen in context, given that there is no evidence of prior systematic antipathy towards Muslims such that it was appreciably greater than for other religious-ethnic minority groups. Part of the explanation, therefore, of a degree of increased scrutiny of Muslims since 7/7 is that actual and planned terrorist attacks have overwhelmingly been the work of Islamists. Had such attacks been planned and carried out by those of another religious-ethnic minority say, for example, by Sikhs, then we would expect Sikhs, rather than Muslims, to be more the object of suspicion and scrutiny; and perhaps Sikh organisations and apologists would have labelled this as 'Sikhophobia'.

I. Examples of the Irish in the 1970s/80s and Blacks up till the present day

In Britain, during the IRA's bombing campaign of the 1970s, there was intense suspicion and harassment of Irish people, especially those from an Irish Catholic background, including the wrongful arrest and imprisonment of innocent Irish people in England (such as 'The Birmingham Six' and 'Guildford Four'). Mary Hickman and Bronwen Walter's research for the Commission for Racial Equality on anti-Irish discrimination provides numerous insightful findings. They point out that anti-Irish hostility was dramatically increased by IRA bombings in Britain – the main changes were:

- Intensification of pre-existing stereotypes portraying all Irish people, from North and South, as violent, mindless terrorists.

- Easier justification of anti-Irish discrimination and racism. It now appeared self-evident that the Irish should be treated with dislike and contempt (Hickman M and Walter B, *Discrimination and the Irish community in Britain, London: Commission for Racial Equality*, 1997, pp. 203–204).

Yet, throughout the 1970s and 1980s, terms such as 'Irish-phobia' or 'Catholophobia' were never deployed to explain state repression of, and hostility towards, the Irish, not even by the Catholic Church and Irish and Catholic civil organisations, or indeed by anti-racist campaigning groups.

Data related to the criminal justice process (stop and search, arrests, cautions, imprisonment) shows that there has long been consistently and proportionally very high rates for all indicators *for Black Afro-Caribbeans:* excepting the searches under the Terrorism Act in 2005/6, they are proportionally far higher than for Asians (data on religion is not available). It therefore seems that rather than Islamophobia, there is *prima facie* evidence of the systematic targeting and harassment of Black people. This could be referred to as an indicator of *Blackophobia* yet, just as with 'Irish-phobia' and 'Catholophobia', this epithet is never used.

II. The Illegitimacy of the APPG's Definition of Islamophobia

The APPG definition of Islamophobia invokes 'Muslimness' as approximating to a race. This is illegitimate given that being a Muslim (just as with any other religion) stems from according with the beliefs and practices of Islam. Race is based on biology: for example, the *Oxford English Dictionary* defines 'race' as 'Each of the major divisions of humankind, having distinct physical characteristics'. As being a Muslim has nothing to do with physical characteristics – indeed Muslims comprise people of all races – it is inappropriate to conflate this with race. Racism is based on biology and has long been, in the main, based on a discriminatory attitude to those of a different skin colour. Similarly anti-Semitism, especially in Europe, has historically been based on the belief that Jews constituted a different race but also that their religion was problematic to dominant Christianity. Given that non-Jews are also Semites, applying anti-Semitism solely to Jews is arguably inappropriate but given that this term has long been in use rather than, for example, 'anti-Jewish prejudice', it has become accepted as solely applying to Jews.

Accordingly, 'Islamophobia' cannot be equated with racism or anti-Semitism: Islam, after all, is an ideology like any other religious or non-religious ideology, as well as a set of practices. Just as we do not refer to 'Buddhistness', 'Hinduness' or 'Sikhness', we should avoid the use of 'Muslimness' in a racialised context.

III. The Need for Evidence

If there is evidence for a higher level of prejudice or hostility towards Islam or Muslims in any sector of society, the causal factors need to be ascertained. For example, evidence would likely find a high degree of hostility to Muslims and Islam in the towns and cities in which child sexual exploitation has been perpetrated by 'grooming gangs', particularly in white working-class communities. It is clear that the overwhelming majority of the perpetrators are Muslim yet there has been far too much silence on this troubling fact – doubtless because those pointing out this reality would be accused of being racists or Islamophobes. This is precisely what happened to Sarah Champion, MP for Rotherham, for stating the truth about the ethnicity and religion of the perpetrators.[2]

This is an entirely false charge and shuts down debate

---

[2] Sarah Champion, 'British Pakistani men ARE raping and exploiting white girls… and it's time we faced up to it', *Sun*, 10 August 2017, available at: https://www.thesun.co.uk/news/4218648/british-pakistani-men-raping-exploiting-white-girls/

and a move towards tackling the problem. Dame Louise Casey in the 2016 *Casey Review on Opportunity and Integration* warned against this by stating:

> Too many public institutions, national and local, state and non-state, have gone so far to accommodate diversity and freedom of expression that they have ignored or even condoned regressive, divisive and harmful cultural and religious practices, for fear of being branded racist or Islamophobic.[3]

This is absolutely correct and her advice should be heeded.

While attention has been focused on Islamic radicalisation and the threat of terror attacks, concerns over Islam are much wider than this as is evidenced by successive surveys. For example, in a chapter for the *British Social Attitudes Survey 2010* David Voas and Rodney Ling (pp. 78-80) found that of all the major religions in Britain, only Islam generated an overall negative response.[4] Similarly, a Populus opinion poll in 2011 (table 96),[5] considered the largest survey into identity and extremism in the UK, found that 52 per cent of respondents agreed with the proposition that 'Muslims create problems in the UK' (a far higher percentage than for other religious groups). Two opinion polls conducted in 2015 (by Survation[6] and YouGov[7]) found that only 22% of the population think that the values of Islam are

---

[3] Dame Louise Casey, 'The Casey Review: A Review into Opportunity and Integration', *Department for Communities and Local Government*, December 2016, available at: https://assets.publishing.service.gov.uk/government/uploads/system/uploads/attachment_data/file/575973/The_Casey_Review_Report.pdf, p. 16.

[4] David Voas and Rodney Ling, 'British Social Attitudes: The 26th Report', 2010

[5] 'Fear and Hope Survey', *Populus*, 2011, available at: http://www.populus.co.uk/wp-content/uploads/2015/12/download_pdf-310111-Searchlight-Fear-and-Hope-survey.pdf

[6] 'British Non-Muslims Poll: Prepared on behalf of Sky News', *Survation*, 20 March 2015, available at: http://survation.com/wp-content/uploads/2015/03/Full-Sky-non-Muslim-tables.pdf

[7] 'Islam and British Values: Survey Results', *YouGov*, 2015, available at: http://cdn.yougov.com/cumulus_uploads/document/ogqzisd2xq/Islam%20and%20British%20values.pdf

compatible with the values of British society. The important point to note is that these views are not a manifestation of Islamophobia but rather are based on concrete Muslim beliefs and practices.

VII. *The Primacy of Freedom of Expression*

A highly problematic aspect of the use of the Islamophobia epithet is that it has long been used to suppress debates, critiques, and criticisms of Islam and Muslims. Hence, this is a fundamental reason why the term should not be given any kind of official imprimatur. Freedom of expression and of speech is a central pillar of liberal democracy and, accordingly, is a right that is enshrined in various laws and agreements. For example, Article 10 of the European Convention on Human Rights (incorporated into UK law in Schedule 1 of the Human Rights Act 1998) states that everyone has the right to freedom of expression.

Likewise, the Parliamentary Assembly of the Council of Europe made clear in Resolution 1510, passed in 2006, that:

> There cannot be a democratic society without the fundamental right to freedom of expression. The progress of society and the development of every individual depend on the possibility of receiving and imparting information and ideas. *This freedom is not only applicable to expressions that are favourably received or regarded as inoffensive but also to those that may shock, offend or disturb the state or any sector of the population,* in accordance with Article 10 of the European Convention on Human Rights (emphasis added).

It is important to note that this resolution was, itself, derived from the Handyside case.[8]

---

[8] See European Court of Human Rights: *Handyside v. The United Kingdom*, 7 December 1976.

Peter Tatchell

The All-Party Parliamentary Group (APPG) on British Muslims has produced a well-intended but worrisome definition of Islamophobia. It states: 'Islamophobia is rooted in racism and is a type of racism that targets expressions of Muslimness or perceived Muslimness.' There are three big problems with this definition.

First, while Islamophobia can be an expression of racism, it is not ipso facto racist because neither Islam nor Muslims are a race. Islam is an idea and Muslims include people from many races.

Second, Muslimness is a vague and subjective term. Who gets to decide what it means? Muslimness means different things even to different sects of Islam – Sunni, Shia, Sufi and Ahmadi. Some ultra conservatives and Islamists claim to represent true Muslimness and use it to justify their opposition to women's and LGBT+ rights.

Third, this definition has implications for free speech. Islam is an idea and like all ideas it should be open to scrutiny and criticism. Yet very often all critiques of Islam are denounced as an attack on Muslim people.

This is unfair. In a free society, it is perfectly valid to criticise the idea of Islam. What is not acceptable is to be prejudiced against Muslim people and to consequently victimise them. Discrimination against ideas is reasonable, but not discrimination against people.

I try to avoid the term Islamophobia. Anti-Muslim hatred is a much better term, since it focuses on prejudice against

Muslim people and their life choices. I speak as someone who has defended the rights of Muslim people for decades but who also defends freedom of expression.

From personal experience, I know how the smear of Islamophobia is used to silence debate and critics. In 1994, I protested against the Islamist extremist group Hizb ut-Tahrir. It endorsed the killing of LGBT people, women who have sex outside of marriage and Muslims who turn away from their faith. I was denounced as Islamophobic. But I was merely confronting the hateful ideology of theocratic Islamism, not Muslim people, the vast majority of whom do not subscribe to such murderous injunctions.

My protest in 1994 could fall within the sweeping definition of Islamophobia proposed by the APPG, since it talks about Muslimness. This is an ambiguous, nebulous term that can cover anything that anyone perceives to be Islamic or Muslim. With this definition in mind, Hizb ut-Tahrir members could say that I am Islamophobic because the sentencing to death of LGBT people, adulterers and apostates is a part of the Islamic tradition – and therefore part of Muslimness.

The APPG definition could be used by Islamists to condemn and refute legitimate criticisms of their extremism. They could use it to argue that any critique of Islam is illegitimate and out of bounds.

No-one in our society should be discriminated against because of who they are. Yet the term Islamophobia downgrades protecting Muslim people and mistakenly puts the focus on protecting ideas. This has to be challenged.

But so far there has been no critique of the APPG's definition by Labour, the Liberal Democrats or the Mayors of London and Manchester. We are, it seems, drifting towards a de facto threat to free speech and liberal values.

Dr David Green

The APPG on British Muslims has proposed the following definition:

> Islamophobia is rooted in racism and is a type of racism that targets expressions of Muslimness or perceived Muslimness.

If this definition became the basis for police action no one would be sure which forms of words could land them in court. It is precisely such uncertainty that makes the difference between a police state and a free society. Historically the term 'rule of law' was used to describe the political system in which everyone knew when the law could be used against them and when they were free to act as each believed best. As the great philosopher Locke, put it, in England there was a 'standing rule to live by, common to every one of that society' which meant, 'A liberty to follow my own will in all things, where the rule prescribes not; and not to be subject to the inconstant, uncertain, unknown, arbitrary will of another'.

The APPG definition would provide a profoundly uncertain rule to live by. At present there is a legal defence of freedom of speech when criticising religions. It was a hard-won amendment to the Racial and Religious Hatred Act of 2006 following a campaign by comedians such as Rowan Atkinson. The Act amended the Public Order Act 1986 by adding the following: 'A person who uses threatening words or behaviour, or displays any written material which is threatening, is guilty of an offence if he intends thereby to stir up religious hatred.' However, section 29J under the heading 'protection of freedom of expression' says:

> Nothing in this Part shall be read or given effect in a way which prohibits or restricts discussion, criticism or expressions of antipathy, dislike, ridicule, insult or abuse of particular religions or the beliefs or practices of their adherents, or of any other belief system or the beliefs or practices of its adherents, or proselytising or urging adherents of a different religion or belief system to cease practising their religion or belief system.

Using words with the intention of stirring up racial hatred is not protected and, no doubt for this reason, the APPG definition claims that criticising Islam is a form of racism. But race and religion are very different. We intuitively dislike being criticised for the things we can't change about ourselves, such as skin colour. In a free society, however, we expect to be criticised for things we can change. And once we are adults we can change our religion, and whether or not we accept all or some of the tenets of the faith to which we belong.

We have here a clash between two very different ways of viewing a society: broadly individualism and collectivism. Individualism focuses on the individual in community. The primary aim of the state is to facilitate development of our personal qualities. It is not the doctrine of an elite fortunate enough to have been born with talents. It has always been egalitarian. The vitally important personal qualities that have been so highly valued are the possession of everyone. We can all choose between being honest or dishonest; hard working or lazy; kind or unkind; public spirited or self-centred; brave or cowardly; determined or weak; resilient or quick to give in; and generous or mean. And we all must decide whether or not to approach others in a spirit of reciprocity or in the hope of gaining one-sided advantage, or to value criticism and engage in self-criticism rather than hold fixed opinions and adopt a righteous stance. These vital choices must be made by all of us and make the difference between a good society and a bad one.

In a collectivist society the aim is for the rulers to determine how individuals should behave. Individuality is not denied. Each must choose between right and wrong, but the rulers lay down a detailed code and threaten punishment for non-compliance. And they do not welcome criticism as a device for mutual learning and holding power to account.

We have encountered these authoritarian ideas throughout the history of Europe and thought we had advanced beyond them. Until modern times no sharp division was made between sin and holding incorrect factual beliefs, such as whether the Sun goes round the Earth. Religious authorities were once seen as the guardians of correct opinions and challenging their doctrines called into doubt their authority. Consequently, they often used the full powers of the state to suppress dissent. In 1600 the Catholic Church burnt Giordano Bruno at the stake in Rome for claiming that the Earth went round the Sun and it forced Galileo to recant similar views in 1632. Open societies in which we try to settle our differences without violence have been a great human achievement and we must be alert to the risk that our precious heritage will be undermined.

The APPG definition is an attempt to recreate the atmosphere of seventeenth-century Rome. The group may not want to burn anyone at the stake, but they do plan to lock people up. Only in 2009 the hotel owners Mr and Mrs Vogelenzang were falsely accused of religious hate crime.

As a result of a conversation with a female Muslim guest, they were accused of a religiously aggravated hate crime and pursued by the police and the Crown Prosecution Service. On the morning in question a Mrs Tazi (who had married a Muslim and converted to Islam) had come down to breakfast wearing traditional Muslim clothes. In the foyer of the hotel she had taken part in a discussion with the hotel owners, Ben and Sharon Vogelenzang, about the respective merits of their religions.

As a result she made a formal complaint to the Merseyside police about what she said were offensive remarks made by the Vogelenzangs about the Muslim prophet Muhammad and Mrs Tazi's Muslim clothes. When the full story came to court, it transpired that a Muslim doctor had also been eating breakfast in the hotel and found nothing objectionable about the Vogelenzang's conduct. His letter was read to the court. He had nothing but praise for the Vogelenzangs: 'I am a Muslim and I know they are devout Christians but… I have never found them to be at all judgemental. They were as friendly with me as with any other guest… Should I need to [stay in Liverpool again] I would not hesitate in again stopping at the Bounty House Hotel.' The doctor said that 'the atmosphere was not at all awkward' (Mrs Tazi claimed that she was being harangued) and that 'if there were any offensive remarks I would have recalled these, as I, being a Muslim myself, would have been offended if anybody mocked my beliefs'. His integrity and courage saved the day. And to speak of courage is no exaggeration. He asked for his name to kept confidential for, amongst other things, fear of retaliation by Muslim extremists. The case was thrown out.

The definition of Islamophobia proposed by the APPG and now being taken seriously by the Home Affairs Select Committee emerges from the same mentality that led

Giordano Bruno to be burnt at the stake, forced Galileo to recant, and put two innocent hotel owners in the dock in 2009 after being hounded for months by the Merseyside police, who put a team of six officers on the case led by a detective chief inspector. There is wide public support for freedom of speech, and it is unlikely to be officially ended by an act of parliament, but it can be chipped away bit by bit, and giving official recognition to the APPG definition of Islamophobia will be a giant step towards an arbitrary police state.

Professor Paul Cliteur

Islamophobia is an impossible construction, and it should make us suspicious of everyone who uses it. Why not call someone a 'sociophobe' when he is critical of socialism? Or someone a 'liberalophobe' when he voices criticism of liberalism? Why no 'atheophobia' when it comes to criticizing the claims of Richard Dawkins, Christopher Hitchens, Sam Harris, and Daniel Dennett? And why is Bertrand Russell's essay *Why I am not a Christian* (1927) not branded as 'Christianophobe'?

As far as I know, phobia discourse has only gained currency in two combinations: homophobia and Islamophobia. It has something to do with identity politics. But whatever it is, let us not fall into the trap of phobia discourse. As people who criticize atheism are not 'atheophobes', people criticizing religion are not ill, as the use of the word phobia implies. The world is full of ideologies, religions, worldviews, points of view, and we should feel free to criticize them.

Tim Dieppe

In November 2018, the All-Party Parliamentary Group (APPG) on British Muslims released a report *Islamophobia Defined*, urging the government to adopt a legal definition of Islamophobia. Certainly, anti-Muslim hatred and discrimination need to be addressed, but the report and its definition are problematic and only likely to make the problem worse. The proposed definition from the APPG is as follows:

> Islamophobia is rooted in racism and is a type of racism that targets expressions of Muslimness or perceived Muslimness.

'Cultural racism'

Tellingly, there is no attempt to define 'Islam' in the APPG report. What they have done instead is racialise Islam so as to make Islamophobia a form of racism. It does not matter that Islam is not a race, or that many Muslims do not see themselves as anything like a separate race. The authors want Islamophobia to be seen as racist. The report explains:

> The concept of racialisation thus situates Islamophobia within anti-racism discourse which is not however just informed by biological race, but by a culture – broadly defined – that is perceived to be inferior to and by the dominant one. (p.39)

The idea is to define 'Islamophobia' as 'cultural racism', making it unacceptable to criticise Islamic culture or practices. By this definition, viewing a culture that gives less rights to women as inferior to one where women have more rights would be Islamophobic. Expressing that it is better for women not to have to cover their faces would also be Islamophobic. Arguing that polygamy should be outlawed because it is bad for society would also be Islamophobic. One would not even be able to say that UK law is preferable to sharia law. Once we agree to the concept of 'cultural racism' and Islamophobia defined in this way, we lose the freedom to criticise Islamic culture.

What is Muslimness?

The definition of Islamophobia hinges on 'Muslimness'. What exactly constitutes 'Muslimness' is left undefined, perhaps deliberately so. The proposed definition of Islamophobia is actually rooted in 'perceived Muslimness', making it entirely subjective. It is not clear whether the 'perceived Muslimness' is perceived by the perpetrator or the victim. Presumably 'Muslimness' is perceived by appearance, though it is not the case that all Muslims wear distinctive clothing.

Sara Khan, Lead Commissioner for Countering Extremism, has written:

> A narrow understanding of 'Muslimness' leaves behind those Muslims who, because of how they choose to live their lives or practise their religion, don't have a 'Muslimness' that other Muslims find acceptable.[1]

This is a stark warning. Ofsted have been accused of Islamophobia for questioning whether young girls should

---

[1] Sara Khan, 'We Are Still Ignoring Victims Of Anti-Muslim Prejudice', *Huffington Post*, 3 December 2018, available at: https://www. huffingtonpost.co.uk/entry/islamophobia-extremism-hate-crime-racism_ uk_5c0566e8e4b066b5cfa475a3

wear the hijab at school (p.55). What about Muslims who do not want their girls to wear the hijab?

It seems that according to this definition, it is impossible for Muslims to be Islamophobic. What about attempts by hard-line Muslims to police the behaviour of others? What about hatred of Muslims for being the wrong type of Muslim? As Sara Khan comments:

> Other Muslims boycott Ahmadiyyah businesses and restaurants, bully Ahmadiyyah children at school, and distribute leaflets calling for their death. If this abuse was experienced by Muslims at the hands of non-Muslims, it would be perceived as anti-Muslim hatred; why should it be any different just because the perpetrators are Muslims themselves?[2]

Who is an Islamophobe?

The list of those who have been accused of being Islamophobic is long and illustrious. For example, there's Theresa May;[3] Tony Blair; Her Majesty's Chief Inspector of Education, Amanda Spielman;[4] Sarah Champion, MP for Rotherham, who spoke out about Islamic grooming gangs;[5] Maajid

---

[2] Ibid.
[3] Shaheen Sattar, 'As a British Muslim, I'm terrified that Theresa May – winner of 2015's Islamophobe of the Year – is my new Prime Minister', *The Independent (Voices)*, 13 July 2016, available at: https://www.independent.co.uk/voices/as-a-british-muslim-im-terrified-that-theresa-may-winner-of-2015s-islamophobe-of-the-year-is-my-new-a7133981.html
[4] Eleanor Busby, 'Teachers accuse Ofsted boss Amanda Spielman of promoting Islamophobia over stance on hijabs in schools', *The Independent*, 1 April 2018, available at: https://www.independent.co.uk/news/education/education-news/ofsted-hijab-ban-islamophobia-schools-amanda-spielman-national-education-union-neu-a8283786.html
[5] Kate McCann, 'Sarah Champion is being used as a 'scapegoat' after warning of cultural link in child sex cases, critics claim', *The Telegraph*, 17 August 2017, available at: https://www.telegraph.co.uk/news/2017/08/17/sarah-champion-used-scapegoat-warning-cultural-link-child-sex/

Nawaz, founder of Quilliam;[6] and Sadiq Kahn, Mayor of London.[7] An accusation of Islamophobia seems to be made against anyone who raises questions about Islamic beliefs or practices. There is no attempt in the APPG report to determine when accusations of Islamophobia would be inappropriate.

The problem with Islamophobia

The Casey Review highlighted the problem with Islamophobia:

> Too many public institutions, national and local, state and non-state, have gone so far to accommodate diversity and freedom of expression that they have ignored or even condoned regressive, divisive and harmful cultural and religious practices, for fear of being branded racist or Islamophobic. …
>
> At its most serious, it might mean public sector leaders ignoring harm or denying abuse.[8]

This is the real problem – fear of being branded Islamophobic. Perhaps we should call this Islamophobiaphobia? At its worst is has meant that public sector institutions have been reluctant to tackle Islamic rape gangs because of Islamophobiaphobia, leaving more girls to be abused.

What about free speech?

The APPG report pays lip service to free speech claiming that it does not intend to curtail free speech or criticism of Islam

---

[6] 'Home Secretary Theresa May voted Islamophobe of the Year', 5 Pillars, 8 March 2015, available at: https://5pillarsuk.com/2015/03/08/home-secretary-theresa-may-voted-islamophobe-of-the-year/

[7] 'Event report: Islamophobia Awards 2018', 27 November 2018, available at: https://www.ihrc.org.uk/activities/event-reports/19489-event-report-islamophobia-awards-2018/

[8] Dame Louise Casey, 'The Casey Review: A Review into Opportunity and Integration', December 2016, available at: https://assets.publishing.service.gov.uk/government/uploads/system/uploads/attachment_data/file/575973/The_Casey_Review_Report.pdf

as a religion (p.11). It noted that many responses focused on the issue of free speech 'with particular emphasis on whether the term is or could be used to silence legitimate criticism of the religion.' (p.34). The National Secular Society objected that "Islamophobia' confuses hatred of, and discrimination against Muslims with criticism of Islam.' (p.34). This is a serious problem. As it stands, people who criticise Islamic teachings, beliefs or practices are often labelled Islamophobic. The report makes no mention of whether criticism of Muhammad should be deemed Islamophobic.

But then the report wants to prohibit criticism of Islam, if that criticism is perceived to be humiliating or marginalising to Muslims:

> As such, the recourse to the notion of free speech and a supposed right to criticise Islam results in nothing more than another subtle form of anti-Muslim racism, whereby the criticism humiliates, marginalises, and stigmatises Muslims. One, real life example of this concerns the issue of 'grooming gangs'.

> Participants reported being told that 'Mohammed is a paedophile', for instance. This comment does not, in a strictly grammatical sense, have the victim themselves as subject, but is rather an example of the 'criticism of Islam' as it is actually articulated and experienced. Yet, clearly, it is aimed at (and can achieve) harm to individual Muslims, and is not rooted in any meaningful theological debate but rather in a racist attempt to 'other' Muslims in general, associating them with the crime our society sees as most abhorrent of all. (p.35)

What is being referred to here, as the report acknowledges, is actually criticism of Muhammad, not of Muslims. It is also criticism of Muhammad that is based on Islamic traditions.[9]

---

9 'ECHR Upholds Penalising Criticism of the 'Prophet of Islam'', *Christian Concern*, 2 November 2018, available at: https://www.christianconcern.com/our-issues/islam/echr-upholds-penalising-criticism-of-the-prophet-of-islam

It appears then that the authors of the report do want to silence criticism of Islam or of Muhammad and that they consider that such criticism *should* be called Islamophobic even if it is rooted in Islamic teaching. This is therefore a flagrant attempt to curtail free speech.

Loyalty to Ummah

Amongst a list of examples of Islamophobia is this one:

> Accusing Muslim citizens of being more loyal to the 'Ummah' (transnational Muslim community) or to their countries of origin, or to the alleged priorities of Muslims worldwide, than to the interests of their own nations. (p.56)

This would mean that the Casey Review would be Islamophobic for reporting:

> We found a growing sense of grievance among sections of the Muslim population, and a stronger sense of identification with the plight of the 'Ummah', or global Muslim community.[10]

Reporting of factual information like this would be censored as Islamophobic under this definition.

Historians threatened

Historian Tom Holland highlighted in a strongly worded twitter thread the problems that the definition would create for historians.[11] Holland has written about the origins of Islam and has been accused of Islamophobia and even received death threats for his work. In one of his tweets he wrote:

---

[10] Dame Louise Casey, 'The Casey Review: A Review into Opportunity and Integration', December 2016.
[11] @holland_tom, Twitter, 15 May 2019, available at: https://twitter.com/holland_tom/status/1128755065844654081

The definition of Islamophobia the Government is being asked to approve is one that threatens to criminalise 'claims of Muslims spreading Islam by the sword or subjugating minority groups under their rule'. But most Muslims, for most of history, would have been fine with these claims.[12]

Other tweets continued:

The definition of Islam we are being given is of a liberalised, westernised Islam – but Islamic civilisation is not to be defined solely by liberal, Western standards. Military conquest & the subjugation of minority groups have absolutely been features of Islamic imperialism.

We risk the ludicrous situation of being able to write without fear of prosecution about the Christian tradition of crusading or anti-semitism, but not the Islamic tradition of jihad or the jizya.[13]

Holland's points need to be taken very seriously indeed.

Police also concerned

An article in *The Times* revealed that another letter to Theresa May had been written by Martin Hewitt, chairman of the National Police Chiefs' Council, warning her that adoption of this definition would hamper counter-terrorism efforts:

Mr Hewitt also tells the prime minister that counterterrorism specialists worry that the definition could lead to judicial review of terror legislation, perhaps rendering even efforts to curb the distribution of extremist material technically Islamophobic. Representatives from counterterror policing,

---

[12] @holland_tom, Twitter, 15 May 2019, available at: https://twitter.com/holland_tom/status/1128756384537956352
[13] @holland_tom, Twitter, 15 May 2019, available at: https://twitter.com/holland_tom/status/1128757203740000256

he notes, were not invited to give evidence to the parliamentary group.[14]

Richard Walton, former Head of Counter-Terrorism Command of the Metropolitan Police has also warned that adopting this definition would *'over time cripple the UK's successful counter-terrorism strategy and counter-terrorism operations.'*

> The APPG definition would thwart the prosecution of individuals for possession of extremist material and dissemination of terrorist publications; even prosecution for membership of (and encouragement of support for) proscribed terrorist groups. Imagine how Anjem Choudary might have used the label 'Islamophobic' in his defence.[15]

The impact of adopting this definition on our security services should not be taken lightly.

The proliferation of phobias

As Christians we believe there is no place for hatred or antagonism towards individuals. When it comes to ideologies or religions, however, freedom of speech requires that we must be able to criticise each other's beliefs in the strongest terms.

There is a problem of competing victimhoods in our society, seen in accusations of homophobia, Islamophobia, transphobia etc, accusations which sometimes have merit, and other times are used to shut down debate. There is no place for racism or for discrimination against individuals

[14] 'The Times View of Islamophobia: Defining Hate', *The Times*, 15 May 2019, available at: https://www.thetimes.co.uk/edition/comment/the-times-view-of-islamophobia-defining-hate-gth73qkml

[15] Richard Walton, 'This Islamophobia Definition Would, if Adopted by Ministers, Pose Problems for National Security', *Conservative Home*, 29 April 2019, available at: https://www.conservativehome.com/platform/2019/04/this-islamophobia-definition-would-if-adopted-by-ministers-pose-problems-for-national-security.html

because of their beliefs. As Christians, we do not want to get into a competition for victim status, so I personally am uncomfortable with the term 'Christianophobia' for similar reasons to my objections to 'Islamophobia'. 'Christianophobia' can also be used to silence criticism of Christianity or of the beliefs and practices of Christians.

No definition needed

The problem with defining 'Islamophobia' is that any definition will not get away from the word being interpreted as encompassing criticism of Islam. The word references 'Islam' rather than 'Muslims' and therefore will always be used in ways which conflate attitudes towards Islam and attitudes towards Muslims.

We already have laws which cover religiously motivated hate crime, incitement to religious hatred, and discrimination because of a person's religion or belief. There is no need to specify a definition of Islamophobia in law. Furthermore, Freedom of Information inquiries have found that some crimes recorded by the police as 'Islamophobic' were actually committed against Christians, Sikhs, Hindus, atheists, and even Jews.[16] This kind of problem will only increase with a legal definition based on perception.

'Anti-Muslim' is a better term

The Network of Sikh organisations, in its submission to the Home Affairs Committee Islamophobia inquiry, said:

---

[16] Richard Walton, 'This Islamophobia Definition Would, if Adopted by Ministers, Pose Problems for National Security', *Conservative Home*, 29 April 2019, available at: https://www.conservativehome.com/platform/2019/04/this-islamophobia-definition-would-if-adopted-by-ministers-pose-problems-for-national-security.html

We are of the view that 'anti-Muslim' hatred (like 'anti-Sikh' or 'anti-Hindu') is much clearer language to describe hate crime specifically against the Muslim community.[17]

One advantage of using 'anti-Muslim' is that it makes clear that it is directed against Muslims as individuals rather than against Islam as a religion. One could also use the term anti-Christian.

Islamic blasphemy law

Defining Islamophobia in law as a form of 'cultural racism' will seriously inhibit free speech. It will protect Islam and Islamic culture from criticism and will create what is in effect an Islamic blasphemy law. We urge the government to resist the pressure to define Islamophobia in law. If Islamophobia is defined according to the APPG report, then the freedom to criticise Islam will be lost.

---

[17] 'Response to Home Affairs Committee Islamophobia Inquiry', *Network of Sikh Organisations*, 28 January 2019, available at http://nsouk.co.uk/response-to-home-affairs-committee-islamophobia-inquiry/

Hardeep Singh

Like for many of my co-religionists, the immediate backlash to 9/11 was a seminal moment. On 15 September 2001, Balbir Singh Sodhi, a gas station owner, was arranging flowers outside his family business in Arizona. He had just returned from Costco, where he purchased some American flags and donated money to a fund for victims of 9/11. Moments later, he was shot dead. Sodhi, a turbaned Sikh, goes down in history as the first person killed in retribution for the Al Qaeda terror attacks. So, 'Islamophobia' was something extending beyond the Muslim community – impacting the 'Muslim looking other' – and Sikhs, like Muslim women in hijabs stood out from the crowd. Sodhi was the first of many Sikhs targeted. In Britain we've had the attempted beheading of dentist Dr Sarandev Singh Bhambra by a member of the now proscribed group National Action (NA) in 'revenge' for Lee Rigby, as well as a former government minister Parmjit Singh Dhanda having a pig's head thrown in his drive – at the time, the former incident was described on Newsnight as 'Islamophobic,' with no mention that Dr Bhambra was in fact a Sikh.

Against this backdrop, and the ongoing marginalisation of Sikhs in government hate crime policy, I was led to question how forces like the MET police were recording so called 'Islamophobic hate crime' in the first place, and whether or not others were (unbeknownst to them) being included in this category, and if so, why was a breakdown not being disclosed by the police or reporting media? Through a number of carefully worded FOIs to the MET police I discovered that significant numbers of non-Muslims and those of no recorded faith were in fact being logged as victims of 'Islamophobic hate crime', (28% for 2015 & 25% for 2016) but these victims were not being acknowledged in police statistics (e.g the Metropolitan police hate crime dashboard) or in media reports of 'hikes' or 'spikes' in hate crime against Muslims in London. They included Christians, Hindus, Sikhs, Buddhists, atheists and even Jews. So, the public perception of hate crime against Muslims was being inflated beyond the reality, and many victims were 'invisible' – and not even given the dignity of being a statistic.

It was for these reasons that our charity, under the leadership of Lord Singh of Wimbledon, chose to engage with this important issue and push back against what we view as the government's 'Abrahamic centric' hate crime action plan. We have since submitted evidence to the Home Affairs Select Committee on hate crime and its violent consequences and more recently to the APPG on British Muslims. On the latter, we have concerns about the proposed APPG definition:

(1) The problem with the word 'Islamophobia' and reference to 'racism' and this new adjective 'Muslimness'

(2) The issue of freedom to discuss matters of public interest and free speech and the consequences for academia, journalism and wider public debate

(3) The impact on national security, counter-extremism work and policing

The problem with the word 'Islamophobia' and reference to 'racism' and 'Muslimness'

To begin with, the term 'Islamophobia' is far too vague. The Freedom of Information Requests I previously referred to support this, highlighting the problem with the word, and the ambiguity of categorising perception-based hate. I see 'Islamophobia' as more of an amalgam or umbrella term – which could be interpreted in several ways, as:

(1) Anti-Muslim hate crime – like the terror attack in New Zealand or street-based attacks on women with hijabs

(2) Hate crime against those perceived to be Muslims or as I previously described the 'Muslim looking other' – my co-author & I have also referred this in our forthcoming book as 'mistaken identity'

(3) A term weaponised by extremists to shut down criticism of aspects of Islamic doctrine or the behaviour of a minority of Muslims – for example Britain's 'grooming gang' phenomenon.

The racist component of the definition is also problematic. As Trevor Phillips has pointed out, 'Muslims themselves rejected the idea that they constitute anything like a single separate 'race' in the way that, say, black Africans might. In fact, it is a central tenet of Islam that all who submit to the faith are equal in the eyes of God irrespective of origin, ethnicity or geography.' The concept of a pan global religious brotherhood or *ummah* that transcends race, borders and nationality is something that my Muslim friends are proud of. I agree with Phillips on this point but would add that by conflating race and religion, the definition serves to furthermore marginalise converts or white Muslims – like Bosniaks, Albanians and Kosovars.

Moreover, it's absurd to suggest 'Islamophobia' is 'a racism', especially when white hipsters with beards (be they Brits or Swedes) have been confused with ISIS. The 2015 case in Sweden related to members of a charitable group called 'bearded villains'[1]. Their ignominy had nothing to do with race, but their hirsute countenance – so I guess we could describe it as 'Islamophobia triggered by pogonophobia', if one chooses to make things especially complicated. But we must keep things simple, and such 'mistaken identity' incidents – like with turbaned Sikhs – suggest a conflation with the attire (or appearance) of extremist Muslims, not racism.

Furthermore, I'd argue the adjective 'Muslimness' in the APPG's definition is also unhelpful, because it serves to expand the framework of anti-Muslim hate to 'expressions' of religious adherence or practice. As far as I can see, there are no attempts in the report to differentiate the 'Muslimness' of Islamists from liberal and reformist Muslim voices. The latter would indeed suffer if this definition is adopted, especially those pushing back against gender segregation or forced hijab wearing. Another difficulty is who decides what qualifies as 'Muslimness', and here the APPG report fails to consider let alone grasp the nettle of persecution of Ahmadiyyas and other minority sects – (during a House of Lords debate in December 2018, Baroness Falkner of Margravine highlighted their plight at the hands of other Muslims).[2] They are not considered by some to have the

---

[1] 'Bearded hipster group says police mistook them for Islamic State terrorists', *Guardian*, 13 October 2015, available at: https://www.theguardian.com/world/2015/oct/13/police-called-as-bearded-hipster-group-mistaken-for-islamic-state-terrorists

[2] Islamophobia debate, House of Lords Hansard, 20 December 2018, available at: https://hansard.parliament.uk/Lords/2018-12-20/debates/2F954D45-1962-4256-A492-22EBF6AEF8F0/Islamophobia

appropriate level of 'Muslimness'. It goes without saying that I'd worry if self-appointed representatives in my community would volunteer to adjudicate my level of 'Sikhness' on behalf of the state too – perhaps the length of my *kirpan* or beard isn't quite long enough, or for those with fringe interests, like promotion of the idiotic notion that Sikhs are an ethnic group, they already label me the wrong kind of Sikh for simply opposing their separatist agenda. Left in the hands of self-appointed 'community leaders', we will be at the mercy of potentially the same voices who are seeking to weaponize this definition, and those who already denounce the government's counter extremism strategy as 'institutionally Islamophobic.'

Freedom to discuss matters of public interest and free speech and the consequences for academia, journalism and debate

On this, I will focus on two specific areas, not because they are higher or lower in the hierarchy of importance, but because they impact me personally: namely the areas of journalism and history. Firstly, journalists who have chosen specificity when describing the background of perpetrators in cases like Rotherham and Rochdale have been labelled as 'Islamophobic'. I've been on the sharp end of this – and rather unhelpfully been referred to as an 'uncle Tom bigot' in addition to 'a member of the BNP' amongst other pleasantries along the way.

In my view, we must surely pay attention to what the victims themselves say. Writing under a pseudonym (Ella Hill) a Rotherham survivor writes: 'As grooming victims, my friends and I were called vile racist names such as 'white trash' and 'kaffir girl' as we were raped. Our Sikh and Hindu friends who were also targeted by Muslim

Pakistani gangs were disparagingly called 'kaffir slags' too.'[3] Now in the context of the APPG definition, she goes on to suggest a definition for the kind of hatred and abuse she suffered: 'Non-Muslim hate is rooted in racism, and is a fear, hatred or hostility towards non-Muslims or those with a perceived lack of Muslimness.'[4] As unpalatable and difficult these conversations are to have, we cannot simply shy away from the hatred that has motivated crimes against victims like Ella, for fear of being labelled 'Islamophobic' – if we do, we will give oxygen to the far right who will use this to deliberately smear the majority law abiding British Pakistani Muslim community. I'm concerned that if this definition is approved, victims and journalists will be silenced. This includes those who expose Islamism or investigate 'entryism' or cases like the Birmingham trojan horse affair. I believe this is a retrograde step for a free, open and civil society. *Islamophobia Defined* incidentally makes four references to grooming gangs, but it makes no effort to examine the motivations of the perpetrators. Instead, it suggests that discussion of grooming gangs could be 'Islamophobic'.

Another group who will be in difficulty are historians. That includes citizen historians like me. I'm sure there are a few others in the room here today. To illustrate why, according to the APPG report, 'claims of Muslims spreading Islam by the sword or subjugating minority groups under their rule' may be 'Islamophobic'. But this could censor discussion of historical facts, such as the more gruesome aspects of the Mughal and Ottoman Empires or Moor conquests, not to

---

[3] 'As a survivor of the Rotherham grooming gang, I am scared by racism and hate crime post Brexit', *Independent*, 4 December 2018, available at: https://www.independent.co.uk/voices/brexit-deal-racism-hate-crime-rotherhamgrooming-gang-child-sex-abuse-islamophobia-definition-a8666416.html

[4] Ibid.

mention the crimes of modern-day ISIS. This is especially worrying for me as a Sikh. Sikhism evolved into a military religion following the martyrdom of our fifth Guru, Guru Arjan. It was later codified into a military fraternity in response to the execution by beheading of Guru Tegh Bahadur (our ninth Guru), who stood up to the forced conversion of Hindu priests in Kashmir by India's Muslim invaders.

Today in Britain, we have images of the two Gurus being executed along with countless other historical *shaheeds* (or martyrs) in gurdwaras up and down the country – could these images be deemed 'Islamophobic' if this definition is passed? I hope not – but you can see where the APPG's agenda could potentially lead us. The truth is these historical events demonstrate periods in which Islam was spread by the sword – but that's not to say all Muslims at the time agreed with this barbarity (or do today). In fact we celebrate the Sufi saint Mia Mir, a close friend of Guru Arjan who laid the foundation stone to our holiest shrine the Golden Temple, or *Harmander Sahib* in Amritsar. Guru Arjan also included the writing of Muslim and Hindu saints in the *Guru Granth Sahib* (the principle scripture of Sikhism) to emphasize that no one faith has the monopoly on truth.

The impact on national security, counter-extremism and policing

I won't be saying much on this, but will refer to the words of former Head of Counter-Terrorism Command of the Metropolitan Police Richard Walton, who has recently gone on record to say:

'It is my firm view that this deeply flawed definition – which wrongly conflates the religion of Islam with a racial group – could over time cripple the UK's successful counter-terrorism strategy and counter-terrorism operations.'[5]

I think politicians need to urgently heed Walton's words, and not give our enemies the opportunity to smear and potentially hinder the critically important work of those tasked with protecting Britain's security, and ultimately protecting our lives. It is for all these reasons I believe the proposed definition is vague, expansive and deeply problematic, and if implemented by well-meaning (but naïve) politicians, will in the words of Dr Qanta Ahmed be inevitably used by Islamists 'as a political and judicial shield to protect them and defame their critics.'[6]

---

[5] Richard Walton, 'This Islamophobia definition would, if adopted by Ministers, pose problems for national security', Conservative Home, 29 April 2019, available at: https://www.conservativehome.com/platform/2019/04/this-islamophobia-definition-would-if-adopted-by-ministers-pose-problems-for-national-security.html

[6] Edward Faulks, 'Adopting the new Islamophobia definition would be terrible for the Tories', Spectator, 4 April 2019, available at: https://blogs.spectator.co.uk/2019/04/adopting-the-new-islamophobiadefinition-would-be-terrible-for-the-tories/

Pragna Patel

For almost 40 years, Southall Black Sisters has provided advocacy and support to black and minority (BME) women who make up some of the most marginalised and powerless sections of our society. Women from Muslim backgrounds make up the largest group of our users, and like other women, arrive at SBS having experienced all forms of gender-based violence and related problems of racism, homelessness, mental illness, trauma, poverty and insecure immigration status. The bulk of our work is directed at assisting BME women and children in obtaining effective protection and to assist them in asserting their fundamental human rights and freedoms. Through advice and advocacy, we assist on average 3500 women a year to obtain immediate protection and access to housing, welfare and mental health services and legal advice and representation in family, immigration, criminal, community care and other legal proceedings. Our work by its very nature addresses issues of multiple or intersectional discrimination, involving the simultaneous experience of race, gender and other forms of inequality. Although based in West London, we have a national and international reach.

Since our inception in 1979, mobilised by the clashes between anti-racist youth and fascists in Southall, we have been vocal in the fight against racism, intolerance and xenophobia. For almost 40 years, we have addressed both internal (cultural and religious) as well as external (racism and structural inequality) constraints that have prevented women from accessing their right to equality and justice. This has involved challenging racist assumptions, stereotypes, laws policies and institutional practices that have only served to heighten the discrimination and marginalisation of all BME people but women in particular as they have the least political power to make their voices heard. We therefore have considerable experience in tackling institutional and everyday forms of racism.

We stress however, that the challenge of racism has not deterred us from also robustly criticising internal 'cultural', 'religious' or 'traditional' practices that have been used to undermine the fundamental human rights of minority women and children. This has sometimes brought us into conflict with both the political and ideological Left and Right; ironically both have accused us of playing into the hands of racists. Our view is that is it not possible to prioritise some struggles against injustice and discrimination and not others. We have instead chosen a path that challenges all forms of discrimination, exclusion and marginalisation, simultaneously, irrespective of how complex and difficult that may be. To do otherwise is to be selective about and complicit in certain forms of injustice and discrimination and not others.

This APPG consultation seems to stem from a question asked of the Parliamentary Under-Secretary of State for Communities and Local Government Lord Bourne, by Baroness Warsi (chair of the APPG) on 17 October 2017 in the House of Lords. She asked Her Majesty's Government 'whether they have a definition of Islamophobia; and, if so, what it is'. Lord Bourne made clear that whilst hatred and intolerance of Muslims had no place in society and that criminal offences motivated by a person's (actual or perceived) religion may amount to a religious hate crime, there was no definition of Islamophobia which was currently endorsed by the Government. Baroness Warsi then asked the Minister 'whether he agrees that it is high time to have a definition of Islamophobia, and that to fundamentally challenge the hate that underpins hate crime, we need to define what that hate is'. She invited the Minister to meet with the APPG, which he agreed to do.

Our concerns in summary

It is always timely to have a discussion on racism and its causes and consequences, particularly in the current climate in which the debate on Brexit and the government's 'hostile climate' on immigration has led to the rise in racial attacks and anti-immigration and xenophobic sentiments. But we question the necessity or utility of defining 'Islamophobia' since it raises vital questions as to whether it is a sufficiently distinct social phenomenon from the reality of racism and discrimination faced by many minorities.

After careful consideration, we have decided not to address the specific questions raised by the APPG call for evidence since they are based on the presumptions that 'Islamophobia' can and should be defined and that to do so would resolve the problems of racism and intolerance towards Muslims. These are presumptions that we cannot agree with for the reasons set out below.

In this submission we highlight some of the fundamental difficulties underlying the issue of 'defining' 'Islamophobia' and offer alternative ways forward. We absolutely acknowledge that Muslims (along with a range of other minority groups) are victims of racism, bigotry and hate crimes. A hate crime which is defined by the Crown Prosecution Service (CPS) as 'any criminal offence which is perceived, by the victim or any other person, to be motivated by a hostility or prejudice' based on one of five categories: religion, faith or belief; race, ethnicity or nationality; sexual orientation; disability; or gender identity.

Anti-Muslim racism is a daily reality for many Muslims in Britain today. This deserves to be robustly addressed as do all hate crimes rooted in racism. However, we are concerned with what appears to be a conflation of racism with the term 'Islamophobia' which in our view does not capture the reality of the discrimination that many Muslims face. We accept that the term is widely used to mean a range of things from the targeting of Muslims on the basis of their religious identity to the stereotyping and open hostility towards Muslims by the media and right-wing groups. But that does not, in our view, make the term any the less problematic. As an organisation that works with vulnerable BME women from all minority backgrounds, we are alert to the ways in which racism plays out in women's lives in particular, and how it combines with other sources of inequality and powerlessness such as patriarchal norms and structures to create formidable barriers to the enjoyment of fundamental freedoms, rights and equality in British society. However, our research and casework has shown that for most of these women, the solution to the problem of racism, inequality and oppression lies not in adopting a religious framework as a countering mechanism, but through the endorsement and application of universal equality and human rights-based laws and norms. Our concern is that adopting a religious framework has, amongst other things, consequences for their right to challenge practices such as domestic violence which necessarily involves challenging religious and cultural injunctions and values.

We have a number of specific concerns in relation to defining 'Islamophobia' that can be summarised as follows:

a. Islamophobia is conceptually impossible to define as it is highly subjective as an idea;

b. Even the most liberal or careful definition still risks conflating the issues of racism, intolerance, and infringement of the religious freedom of individuals with criticism of religion itself;

c. There are serious concerns that a definition could infringe on free speech.

In our view, incidents which amount to racism and discrimination can and must be dealt with under the appropriate existing legislation such as that on hate crimes (coupled with better understanding and more effective use of criminal and civil legislation by the police, prosecutors and courts). We view this as a more helpful approach rather than creating a new and contentious definition which we fear will do little to combat racism and instead will add to the confusion and uncertainty that already exists. More crucially, it has the potential to be used to silence and censor genuine criticism of religion and religious practices.

The solution to the problem of racism should be addressed by improving the current legal framework, rather than by creating a specific definition of 'Islamophobia' that will raise more problems than it will solve.

Our concerns in detail
I. Islamophobia is conceptually impossible to define
The meaning of the term 'Islamophobia' is not settled and means different things to different constituencies even within Muslim populations.

The ambiguity of the very term is not surprising since there is considerable confusion as to how the term first arose. Commentators have noted that even the origin of the term 'Islamophobia' is disputed. UK sources attribute its popularisation to a 1997 publication by the Runnymede Trust *(Islamophobia: A Challenge for Us All)*, which itself referred to the first usage being in a February 1991 in article in the US periodical *Insight*. The Runnymede report accepted the word was not 'ideal' but considered it a '… useful shorthand way of referring to dread or hatred of Islam – and, therefore, to fear or dislike all or most Muslims….Within Britain it means that Muslims are excluded from the economic, social and public life of the nation….'.

However, French sources trace the origin of the term to the Ayatollah Khomeini and Iranian fundamentalists, who declared Islam inviolate and who said Iranian women who rejected the veil were 'Islamophobic' (Meredith Tax, 'Unpacking the Idea of "Islamophobia"', *Open Democracy*, 20 May 2013). In other words, this was a means by which to assert a totalitarian agenda and was deliberately unspecific as to whether it refers to a religion, a belief system or its faithful adherents around the world.

Tax further notes that the ambiguities in usage reflect these contradictory sources, one anti-racist, the other Islamist. She goes on to say that we are currently in a linguistic minefield.

Even a literal definition of 'Islamophobia' is problematic. A 'phobia' is in fact an 'irrational fear' or mental disorder. Clearly, the levels of racism towards Muslims in the UK and indeed in Europe and the US (referred to further below) cannot be reduced to mental illness. As Tax notes, to do so is to de-politicise the issue. She considers such campaigns to be part of a calculated demagogy. We agree. The nature and levels of discrimination and crimes of hate perpetrated against Muslims by racists and far right groups are deliberate and calculated acts of racism and racial violence – not acts borne out of irrational fear.

The term also pre-supposes that there is a homogeneous group of Muslims who are defined only by their religion and who all consent to a singular version of Islam that must be protected from any criticism. The reality is that there is no such thing as a 'Muslim community' or 'Muslim voice' but many different groups of Muslims whose backgrounds, views and identities range from being secular and feminist to conservative and fundamentalist. Even a widely accepted definition will not suffice since there is ambiguity in the very practice and in the range of meanings that depend very much on the political positioning of the person making the claim. The term does not lend itself to a consistent and coherent approach and its very use stems from varying ideological histories and positions. It is as much likely to support those engaged in censorship as it is those seeking to combat racism, as we explain below.

II. Islamophobia conflates too many issues

We would emphasise that even a widely accepted or highly liberal definition of 'Islamophobia' would not work; the term is riddled with ambiguities and conflates too many issues since it implies not just hatred of Muslims but of the religion itself. To liberals, it can mean discrimination and hate crimes but to fundamentalists it means an attack on religious Islamic texts and precepts or the 'offense of religious sensibilities' for which the only punishment is censorship, violence and even death.

To this end, the term has been conveniently used by Muslim fundamentalists and ultra-conservatives to clamp down on any kind of internal questioning or dissent from religious and community norms as defined by the most powerful and dominant illiberal forces in minority communities. The most dramatic example of this was the endorsement of the Ayatollah Khomeini's' call for the death of Salman Rushdie in 1989 by various Muslim leaderships in the UK who monopolised the so called 'Muslim' voice through the use of intimidation and fear. They left no space for liberal, secular, feminist and atheist Muslims who questioned the fatwa and religious censorship. Indeed the term 'Islamophobia' was used by the academic Moddod to mount an attack on Rushdie's The Satanic Verses, arguing that it was 'a deliberate, mercenary act of Islamophobia' (Moddod, T., 'British Asian Muslims and the Rushdie Affair', The Political Quarterly, Volume 61(2), April 1990). Another more recent example is the killing of Asad Shah, an Ahmadi Muslim living in Scotland, who was deemed by his killer to have 'blasphemed' against Islam and 'disrespected' the Prophet Muhammed.[1]

Those who challenge and criticise community norms, including SBS itself, have been labelled 'Islamophobic'. This then creates a climate conducive to ridicule and even violence against those who dissent; many have been subject to hatred and threats for criticising religious norms and that are deemed to be 'offensive'. For example, the extremist and fundamentalist linked organisation Cage, described the intervention of SBS and the organisation Inspire in a gender segregation case involving a co-ed faith based school (HM Chief Inspector of Education, *Children's Services and Skills v The Interim Executive Board of Al-Hijrah School* [2017] EWCA Civ 1426) as 'Islamophobic' and essentially accused

---

[1] Severin Carrell, 'Man who murdered Glasgow shopkeeper Asad Shah in sectarian attack jailed', *Guardian*, 9 August 2016, available at: https://www.theguardian.com/uk-news/2016/aug/09/tanveer-ahmed-jailed-for-murder-glasgow-shopkeeper-in-sectarian-attack

us of following the 'Prevent' agenda.[2] The point of such accusations is to create a climate that legitimates hostility, aggression and abuse against those who dare to question religious precepts.

Do our challenges and criticisms of fundamentalist and ultra-conservative interpretations and practices of Islam that undermine the rights of vulnerable Muslim women and girls in particular make us Islamophobic? Are those who are secular Muslims or gay Muslims or those who are not deemed to be Muslims (Ahmadis) or those who no longer wish to practice Islam, also Islamophobic? The reality is that those who call themselves secular, atheist or 'Ex-Muslims' already face considerable death threats and abuse from fundamentalists for being 'apostates' and 'heretics' for which the penalty in Islam is death. (See the case of Asad Shah cited above) As it is, we are concerned that hate crimes perpetrated towards such groups by fundamentalists and extremists are even now conveniently ignored by the police and prosecutorial services precisely because the dominant understanding of 'Islamophobia' as defined by fundamentalists and conservatives precludes this. Yet the irony is that these are the very groups that are likely to be highly vulnerable to the charge of 'Islamophobia' and therefore to calls for their prosecution. It is important to note that powerful conservative and fundamentalist Muslim leaderships and organisations are more likely to lead an unchallenged charge of 'Islamophobia' since they are the dominant voice and have power to define the term within the various Muslim populations in the UK

---

[2] 'Outlawing gender segregation: How PREVENT and Ofsted are about conditioning our children, neo-con style', *CAGE*, 29 October 2017, available at: https://cage.ngo/article/outlawing-gender-segregation-how-prevent-and-ofsted-are-about-conditioning-our-children-neo-con-style/

Even a more liberal definition such as the original definition of Islamophobia proposed by the Runnymede Trust (the '...dread or hatred of Islam – and, therefore, to fear or dislike all or most Muslims....' Within Britain it means that Muslims are excluded from the economic, social and public life of the nation....') is significantly problematic, since it collapses any criticism of Islam with discrimination and hate crimes against Muslims. We would strongly argue that there is no causal relationship between dread of Islam and fear or dislike of all Muslims or their exclusion from public life. Our concern is that artists, writers and groups like SBS or 'The Council of Ex-Muslims of Britain', who criticise religion or experiences of oppression attributable to the values of that religion are as likely to be caught by this definition than those who propagate anti-Muslim racism.

The more recent short-form definition put forward by the Runnymede Trust (*Islamophobia: Still a Challenge for Us All – a 20th anniversary report*, November 2017) which simply states that 'Islamophobia is anti-Muslim racism' begs the question: why not address the problem as anti-Muslim racism then? What does the term 'Islamophobia' add?

Clearly the term 'Islamophobia' conflates racism with the legitimate and democratic right to question and challenge religious values that undermine other fundamental rights and freedoms, especially of minorities within minorities. This is not simply a question of semantics since how the problem of anti-Muslim racism is conceptualised will have real consequences for how it is addressed. Even those who have promoted the concept of 'Islamophobia' acknowledge that the term is deeply problematic in respect of how it is addressed.

A careful analysis of mainstream press reports of 'Islamophobic incidents', reveals that they are in reality racially or religiously motivated hate crimes for which legislation already exists. The following are some examples:

a. Darren Osborne, who was convicted of the Finsbury Park mosque attack on 19 June 2017, was said to be motivated (variously) by the idea that all Muslims were rapists; that there were too many terrorists on the street and that 'raping, inbred bastards' needed to 'get back to the desert' (Independent 23 January 2018);

b. Paul Moore was convicted of attempted murder, grievous bodily harm and dangerous driving for running over a Muslim woman and driving his car at a 12-year-old girl as 'revenge' for terror attacks and said he was 'doing his country a favour.' (Independent 2 March 2018)

c. On 7 March 2018, a couple associated with the far-right group Britain First were convicted for carrying out anti-Muslim attacks on those they wrongly believed to be defendants in an ongoing rape trial. The presiding judge stated that 'It was a campaign to draw attention to the race, religion and immigrant background of the defendants.'[3]

d. A Sikh man waiting in the security queue to enter Parliament had his turban ripped off by an assailant shouting 'Muslim go back.'[4]

These are clear examples of crimes motivated by anti-Muslim racism, which is increasingly also linked to anti-immigration

---

[3] Lizzie Dearden, 'Britain First leaders jailed for anti-Muslim hate crime', *The Independent*, 7 March 2018, available at: https://www.independent.co.uk/news/uk/crime/paul-golding-jayda-fransen-britain-first-leaders-guilty-religious-muslim-hate-crime-a8244161.html

[4] Tom Batchelor, 'Sikh man has turban ripped off in racist attack while waiting to meet MP outside Parliament', *Independent*, 22 February 2018, available at: https://www.independent.co.uk/news/uk/crime/sikh-man-turban-ripped-off-parliament-hate-crime-police-london-portcullis-house-a8222376.html

hostility and hatred towards people of a different colour, ethnicity or culture. As the final example above shows, even people of Hindu, Sikh and other South Asian backgrounds and their institutions have also been targeted and attacked in the name of anti-Muslim hatred, but which is in fact aimed at anyone that is foreign and looks the wrong colour (see for example, Peter Hopkins, Katherine Botterill, Gurchathen Sanghera & Rowena Arshad, 'Encountering Misrecognition: Being Mistaken for Being Muslim', *Annals of the American Association of Geographers, 107:4, 934-948* 2017) which looked at the experiences of young Scottish people subjected to abuse for 'appearing' Muslim). The misrecognition issue also raises another problem: are attacks against minorities for supposedly being Muslim to be prosecuted as crimes motivated by Islamophobia or are such experiences better categorised as racially motivated crimes? The phenomenon of 'Islamophobia' is therefore better captured by the traditional lens of racism.

It is notable that hate crimes against Muslims soared at the same time as the 2016 EU referendum due to the widespread anti-immigration sentiments that were stoked by a toxic and hostile rhetoric calling for the need to 'take our country back' (Evening Standard, 2018).[5] Figures released after the 23 June 2016 EU referendum reveal that 3,192 hate crimes were reported to police in England and Wales in the two weeks either side of the referendum – a 42 per cent increase from the same period in the previous year. A further 3,001 hate crimes were reported between 1 and 14 July, mainly by members of minority ethnic and faith communities, new

---

[5]   Robin De Beyer, 'Revealed: Anti-Muslim hate crimes in London soared by 40% in a year', *Evening Standard*, 26 February 2018, available at: https://www.standard.co.uk/news/crime/revealed-antimuslim-hate-crimes-in-london-soared-by-40-in-a-year-a3775751.html

migrants, asylum seekers and refugees ('*Tackling Hate Crime in the UK*' – Amnesty International).[6]

Clearly the anti-immigration sentiments were pervasive; giving a licence to the display of all forms of racism: 'The issue of immigration was at the fore and scaremongering seemed to fuel and legitimise hostility towards minority ethnic and faith communities' (Amnesty International, cited above).

Looking at the wider picture, according to the Home Office the number of hate crimes in England and Wales increased by 29% from 62,518 in 2015/2016 to 80,393 offences in 2016-17 – the largest increase since the Home Office began recording figures in 2011-12. 78% of the offences related to racial hatred and 7% to religious hate. Although some of this may be due to better crime recording and increased reporting, the figures showed rises after the Westminster Bridge, Manchester Arena and London Bridge attacks in 2017. The data also showed that racially or religiously aggravated offences were more likely to be dealt with by a charge/summons than their non-aggravated counterpart offences (Home Office – Hate Crime, England and Wales 2016/2017 – Statistical Bulletin 17/17, 17 October 2017).

In our view, the above demonstrates that it would be a grave mistake to institutionalise the term 'Islamophobia' to reflect what is in essence racism (consisting of prejudice, discrimination and even violent attacks on immigrants, Muslims, and other minority groups). These can all be effectively addressed through existing criminal and equality laws that are themselves the products of anti-racist struggles.

We believe that the correct term to use is anti-Muslim racism. Much in the same way that we have recently seen a rise in anti-immigration racism, anti- Muslim racism is part

---

[6] 'Tackling hate crime in the UK', *Amnesty International*, available at: https://www.amnesty.org.uk/files/Against-Hate-Briefing-AIUK.pdf

of the continuum of racism that must be fought together. But because the term 'Islamophobia' echoes the worldview of the Muslim Right, it does more to confuse the issues than clarify them. More importantly, it does more to harm the cause of anti-racism precisely because the fundamentalist agenda is antithetical to equality and human rights principles including the right to freedom of expression.

III. Consequences for free speech

Attempts to tackle racism and hate crime must be robust but should not fall into the error of suppressing freedom of expression. The European Convention on Human Rights (ECHR) enshrines the right to freedom of expression under article 10, and protects not only 'information' or 'ideas' that are favourably received or regarded as inoffensive or as a matter of indifference, but also those that offend, shock or disturb the State or any sector of the population. Article 10(2) permits restrictions so long as they are prescribed by law, necessary in a democratic society, in pursuit of a legitimate aim, and proportionate to that legitimate aim. The European Court of Human Rights has held in *Kokkinakis v. Greece* of 25 May 1993 (Series A no. 260-A) and a number of subsequent cases that the State has a responsibility to ensure the peaceful enjoyment of the right guaranteed under Article 9 ECHR to the holders of those beliefs and doctrines. In extreme cases the effect of particular methods of opposing or denying religious beliefs can be such as to inhibit people from exercising their freedom to hold and express them. However, the Court has also clearly stated that those who choose to exercise the freedom to manifest their religion cannot reasonably expect to be exempt from all criticism. They must tolerate and accept the denial by others of their religious beliefs and even the propagation by others of doctrines hostile to their faith.

It should also be noted that article 17 ECHR amounts to a prohibition on the abuse of Convention rights. It has been relied on by the Court to exclude hate speech (encouraging for example racial or religious hatred which negates the fundamental values of the ECHR), from the protection of the ECHR, e.g. *Norwood v UK* (admissibility decision of 16 November 2004, 23131/03).

We are concerned that the existing interpretation of 'Islamophobia' would fall foul of article 10(2). How does one identify and describe legitimate criticisms or anxieties on the one hand and hate-filled or irrational criticisms and anxieties on the other? Would the following be considered Islamophobic: a condemnation of political Islam; criticism of patriarchal and heterosexual structures inherent in Islam; criticism of 'sharia laws' and gender segregation; criticism of prominent Muslim leaders; the promotion of atheism and secularism? We would argue that these are all legitimate expressions of free speech that should be protected by article 10(1) but may be caught by a definition of 'Islamophobia'. The point is that in a climate of fundamentalism and religious intolerance in all religions, it would be easy for state agencies such as the police to cave into demands for the arrest and prosecution of those deemed to have 'offended religious sensibilities' for fear of being labelled 'Islamophobic' or 'offensive'. We know this only too well from our own work in challenging cultural and religious practices such as FGM, polygamy, forced marriage, honour-based violence and sexual abuse; these issues were once subject to a 'hands off' approach by state services that were more preoccupied with the fear of being labelled racist and causing offence than with protecting vulnerable women and children.

We are concerned that entrenching and legitimating the term 'Islamophobia' will lead to confusion and the censorship of legitimate criticisms and thus infringe on the right to freedom of expression.

The way forward – tackle anti-Muslim racism as racism

Islam is not a race or ethnicity. In literal terms it is a set of religious ideas, criticism of which cannot be conflated with racism towards a group of people. To hold otherwise is absurd and illogical since the attacks against individuals and groups which are labelled 'Islamophobic' are in fact no different to the racism faced by many other minorities.

Sadly the term has become a way of privileging discrimination faced by Muslims when in reality, the same forms of discrimination and racism are faced by other BME groups, who also experience similar or even greater levels of inequality, exclusion and discrimination. For example African-Caribbean groups are disproportionately represented in prisons, care homes and in school exclusions. Immigrants and asylum seekers are particularly subject to vilification and racial attacks. To therefore recognise 'Islamophobia' as a specific discrimination strand is to contribute to the creation of a hierarchy of oppression and victimhood which can become a barrier to solidarity and integration as different groups compete for the right to be seen as the most oppressed and the ultimate type of victims. Our concern is that the adoption of the term not only encourages such a regressive politics of victimhood but prevents solidarity from forming for the purposes of challenging all forms of racisms.

We are also concerned that if the term is institutionalised, other BME populations, namely Hindus and Sikhs, who also face exclusion, marginalisation and inequality, will also seek to have their experiences recognised in accordance with their religious identity; in other words to be defined solely in relation to religion which needs protecting from any polluting or questioning force. The potential for suppression of dissent is the same as in relation to 'Islamophobia'. We have come across Hindus for instance stating that those who dissent or question religious norms are displaying 'Hinduphobic' views. But this label is often used to target those who legitimately question so-called Hindu norms that for example justify caste discrimination or the oppression of women and girls. For example, we point to the ways in which Hindu fundamentalists clamped down on art exhibitions by the Indian artist, MF Hussain in 2006 for 'offending Hindu sensibilities'.[7] See too the ways in which Sikh fundamentalists have sought to ban plays and disrupt inter-faith marriage ceremonies in Sikh temples using violence and intimidation,[8] all in the name of 'protecting' their faith as they have come to define it.

Racism must be seen as a structural phenomenon rooted in political, economic and cultural structures of power. It is an experience that is shared by many minority groups and needs to be challenged in solidarity, rather than in competition, with others. The ECHR already provides protection for those facing Anti-Muslim racism, through provisions of article 9 (when looked at with article 10 and article 17), as set out above.

The existing criminal law of England and Wales also provides redress. We have referred above to the CPS definition of hate crime. The CPS and police also have a joint definition of cases involving 'hostility on the basis of race or religion':

---

[7] 'Reinstate Indian art exhibition', *Guardian*, 29 May 2006, available at: https://www.theguardian.com/theguardian/2006/may/30/1

[8] Dil Neiyyar and Perminder Khatkar, 'Sikh weddings crashed by protesters objecting to mixed faith marriages', *BBC News*, 11th March 2013, available at: http://www.bbc.co.uk/news/uk-21721519

Any incident/crime which is perceived by the victim or any other person, to be motivated by hostility or prejudice based on a person's race or religion or perceived race or religion.

The threshold needed to demonstrate 'hostility' is not high, and the perception of the victim is key.

Offences of wounding, assault, criminal damage, harassment, stalking and threatening/abusive behaviour that are racially or religiously aggravated can already be prosecuted under the Crime and Disorder Act 1998. The Criminal Justice Act 2003 also gives the court power to increase the sentence of any offence (other than those already provided for in the Crime and Disorder Act 1998) which is racially or religiously aggravated. In addition, s17 of the Public Order Act 1986 created offences of stirring up racial hatred through the use of threatening, abusive or insulting words, behaviour or written material. In 2006 and in 2008, this provision was extended to cover incitement on the grounds of religious identity and sexual orientation. This can be used to prosecute serious cases of race or religious hate speech.

The above shows that there is already considerable protection available for victims of racial and religiously motivated hate crime. Certainly, there is evidence that enforcement of that protection is not as effective as it should be. Amnesty International (in their report cited above) recommended a review of the legislation including extending the list of protected characteristics and to provide equal protection for all characteristics. They also recommended that public figures speak out vigorously against racism and hate. Amnesty International's case studies found significant difficulties with the response of the police, prosecutors and the courts who do not take racism seriously. This would chime with our own experiences.

We would support the suggestion made by Amnesty International that public officials who behave in a discriminatory way or use or condone racist or discriminatory language should be held accountable and face clear disciplinary sanctions.

Conclusion

We strongly urge the committee to recognise the principle that rights and protections must be afforded to individuals and not to religions or other belief systems. The term 'Islamophobia' conflates the protection of individuals from racism with the protection of religion from criticism and dissent. Further, by basing the protection on religion affiliation rather than race or migration status, we risk the 'silo-fication' of the struggle against racism and discrimination on racial or religious grounds. Instead we should have one unifying and unified approach – based on principles of anti-discrimination, equality and human rights (including freedom of expression). This framework already exists but needs improving and robust implementation at all levels of the criminal justice system. We would also encourage better guidance for police, prosecutors and judges in investigating, charging, trying and sentencing hate crime cases, and for there to be clear accountability mechanisms for victims when the criminal justice system fails them.

As we have set out at length above, anti-Muslim racism is not the product of an individual phobia or irrational fear of the 'other'. It is a form of racism that has to be tackled politically and legally through inclusive and progressive laws. To do otherwise is to fall into the fundamentalist trap of using religion to promote a regressive agenda of censorship and control.

Ed Husain

As a Muslim, I find the term 'Islamophobia' an etymological fallacy. Islam, by the definition of its founder the Prophet Mohammed and its greatest philosophers (al-Farabi, Ibn Tufayl, Averroes), is considered to be a 'natural way', or religion of the *fitrah*. Humans cannot have a phobia against nature. It is the height of moral insanity for an intelligent Muslim to place the word 'Islam' and the word 'phobia' together in a single phrase. The term 'Islamophobia' was lifted from discrimination against homosexuals: homophobia. The parallels do not stand up to serious scrutiny between Islam as an idea, a faith, a civilisation, and motivator for behaviour, and homosexuality as a private practice of consenting adults that had led to punishment and killings.

How can a society that celebrates Mo Farah, elevates the hijab-donning Nadia Hussain as Her Majesty's baker by popular consent, and vociferously support Mo Salah as our great football player be credibly anti-Muslim or 'Islamophobic'?

We are exaggerating and conflating the notion of 'Islamophobia' with socio-political factors of collectivism, victimhood culture and identity politics in a world in which attitudes are increasingly dominated by the sewage pipes of social media.

The idea of 'Islamophobia' is an oxymoron, but innocent Muslims feeling under attack is a reality in Britain. Tell MAMA

(Measuring Anti-Muslim Attacks) received 608 reports of anti-Muslim crime in the first half of 2018, 45.4% of which was deemed 'abusive behaviour': spitting, ripping women's hijabs, destruction of Muslim property and mosques, and arson. In 2017, 70% of anti-Muslim crimes reported to Tell MAMA were committed in public and elicited a police response.

There is clearly a problem of rising anti-Muslim sentiment in Britain, but how can the shutdown of open societies and freedom of debate through the political correctness by-word 'Islamophobia' address these violent attacks? Individuals in this great country are already protected from being treated less than favourably on the basis of their religion under the 2010 Equality Act. The 2006 Racial and Religious Hatred act makes it a criminal offense to incite hatred against someone one the basis of their religion but crucially states in Part 3A, clause 29J that the Act does not prohibit 'discussion, criticism, or expressions of antipathy' towards particular religions or their adherents.

What has changed since 2006? Why do some members of parliament feel the need to implement the idea of this new 'phobia' in a way that will empower the ideological bullies of Islamism, and limit our rights to discussion and criticism, the hallmarks of a liberal society?

Sensitivity to Islam is driven by fear of terrorism.

The following factors must be borne in mind when seriously investigating 'Islamophobia' in Britain.

Cause and Effect

The generations of Muslims who arrived in Britain in the 1950s, 1960s, and 1970s after the British Nationality Act of 1948 (which opened the country to immigration from the Commonwealth nations) did not complain about

'Islamophobia'. Then, as now, Britain's great people were not inherently bigoted towards others. We forget that this country had just fought on the Continent in defence of a free and liberal world with 2.5 million Muslims who travelled to Europe to fight for Britain.

If the concept of 'Islamophobia' was non-existent for most of the latter half of the twentieth century, why is there now a phobia of open expression in Britain?

The Salman Rushdie affair in 1988 unleashed a challenge to this established order of free enquiry, free thought, and open society in which all ideas are open to scrutiny.

The data suggests that we have forgotten cause and effect: it was the rise of Islamist extremism and its violent cousin, jihadi terrorism, that unleashed a rise in anti-Muslim sentiment in the West. In the United States after 9/11, ordinary Muslims were treated as suspects and tens of thousands were detained or investigated. Preacher Franklin Graham's definition of Islam as a 'religion of war' sunk deep into the nation's consciousness. In the UK in the wake of the 7/7 bombings, hate crimes against British Muslims in the following weeks rose by 573% in comparison to the previous year. Similar trends followed the murder of Lee Rigby in May 2013 (373% higher than the previous year) and Charlie Hebdo (275%).

A Pew Research Poll in 2016 found that 28% of Britons were unfavourable towards Muslims. ComRes in the same year reported that 31% perceived Islam as a violent religion and 43% thought it was a negative force in UK society. These perceptions are direct results of the dominant narrative of Islamist jihadism sensationalised by the media and touted by members of the far right.

We must go after the cause – the dominant narrative of Islamism and jihadism – rather than intimidating ordinary

Muslims, often themselves victims of such fundamentalist bullying. By shouting 'Islamophobia' in the face of those who call for reform, we end the debate on how we can stop religious causes for such violence.

It is activist Muslim organisations, influenced by the political ideology of the Muslim Brotherhood and Jamat-e-Islami (a Marxist form of confrontational Islam known as Islamism) that are driving this narrative of victimhood. They deny the existence of such violent fundamentalism and wish to cast ordinary Muslims in this country as a collective bloc of victims who must rise up against non-Muslim, capitalist oppression. By speaking for the nearly 3 million UK citizens who are Muslim in such a manner, ordinary Muslims' rights to expression are smothered and ignored. These same Muslim activists conveniently forget that the Prophet Mohamed was a capitalist, a Meccan trader.

Moreover, by officially adopting the offense of 'Islamophobia', we open the door to the worst consequences. The German judge who refused to grant a Muslim woman a divorce from her abusive husband in 2007 did so on the grounds that it was culturally acceptable and sanctioned by the Quran. Many more such incidents will become 'normal' for fear of accusations of racism and 'Islamophobia'.

We cannot tolerate the Islamist intolerance of women, gay people, apostates, and reformist Muslims by shutting down all debate and restricting the possibility of criticism and thus the possibility of reform.

We need to target the cause of this problem, not the consequences.

Consequences on Western Civilisation
One impact of adopting any definition of 'Islamophobia' is that we encourage victimhood rather than responsibility.

We burn the bridges of liberty and freedom of expression on which millions of Muslims travelled to the West.

In the middle ages and early modern period, Muslims were viewed by Christians as blasphemers and were barred from settling in this country in significant numbers. Bringing in a new blasphemy law by default will slowly corrode the freedoms on which western society is founded.

To apostatise and proselytize, to offend and embrace, to accept and reject: these are the dualities that uphold the essence of liberty.

The necessity of personal liberty is at the core of modern western civilisation and was made possible only through a long historical process of sacrifice and suffering.

Blasphemers were not burnt at the stake, innocent lives were not cut short by the guillotine, nor were tens of millions of lives lost in the two world wars for us to abandon our hard-won liberty at the first cry of discomfort.

Where would we be today if we had censored David Hume's criticisms of Christianity in the eighteenth century, or banned Gibbon's volumes on the history of Rome in which he condemned the institutionalisation of religion?

Britain's legacy of liberty stretches back nearly a millennium, from the Magna Carta to the early pioneers of religious freedoms during the Reformation, to the adoption of the Human Rights Act in 1998. The great thinkers of the English Reformation and Enlightenment suffered to give rise to the concept of individual freedoms and choice of religion in a time of rigid blasphemy laws. Thomas More petitioned Henry VIII in 1523 for the right of free speech, John Knox led the Scottish Reformation against the staunchly Catholic Mary Queen of Scots, and Locke promoted the rights of individuals to act as they saw fit. These and many others suffered to give rise to a free Protestant nation and prevent laws against thought crimes.

If history has taught us one thing, it is that Inquisitions begin with censoring and formal definitions of political-religious orthodoxy. We, as a society, are the inheritors of the sacrifices of the humanist philosophers. Galileo was imprisoned for his scientific belief. In 1600, Giordano Bruno was burnt at the stake in Rome for denying tenets of Catholic faith and believing in the possibility of life on other planets. The Dutch Jew Baruch Spinoza was shut out of his community and his books placed on the Catholic Index of Forbidden Books for questioning the nature of the Divine. We are the inheritors of these sacrifices and must not squander them through regression by the shutting of open debate.

Mocking the sacred, however distasteful and disturbing to believers of a particular faith or specific tradition, is often the hallmark of innovation and progress. Islam was born because the Prophet Mohammad mocked the religion of the Meccans. Judaism thrived because Abraham and later Moses opposed the pagan Egyptians in their persecution of the Jewish people. Christianity emerged as Paul and the early disciples attacked the values of Rome and the laws of Judea. Jesus himself directly insulted the wickedness, hypocrisy, and ungodliness of the Pharisees in the New Testament.

Offense is a requisite for freedom, and citizens of open societies must learn to become resilient. Criticism and open discussion are the harbingers of progress.

By stopping critiques of Islam in the name of the new orthodoxy of 'Islamophobia' we will be harming the foetus of modern, liberal Islam. At a time when Islam is suffering from poor health, this curtailment of open discussion and criticism will result in the birth of a stillborn baby with all the defects of religious literalism, hatred, anger, and violence that is espoused by fundamentalists who play on the narrative of victimisation. With 30 million Muslims in the West, a historically unprecedented demographic change, our enlightened age demands that we help Muslims through integration, not isolation.

Today it is 'Islamophobia'; tomorrow will it be that we cannot question the gender inequality of literalist Islam, wife beating, unfairness of divorce laws, inheritance disparity, or reactions to apostasy?

After criminalising 'Islamophobia', will we then stop free Muslim women from questioning those who wear the hijab or niqab? Will we ban books by Voltaire or Kipling or Richard Dawkins for their anti-Islam content? I am a Muslim and I am confident that by drawing on the inherent Islamic intellectual arguments for pluralism and rationalism, we can openly discuss and debate with Dawkins, Rushdie, and other critics of my religion. They are saying nothing new – the Prophet Mohammed encountered much worse abuse in his time.

Lawmakers: Rules from Exceptions
On the role of politics, our lawmakers must not draw rules from the exceptions.

'Islamophobia' was designed to mirror the idea of homophobia and drew parallels with anti-Semitism. This argument is inherently flawed as both homophobia and anti-Semitism are based on untruths and are directed against specific peoples. 'Islamophobia' is about ideas, beliefs and attitudes.

There are those who point to anti-Semitism and argue that as our laws protect Jews, so Muslims must have official protection. Aside from the infantile nature of that thought, we must bear in mind the following:

1. The Jewish population in Britain is around 280,000, while the Muslim population is around 3 million. Jews are not an evangelical or proselytizing community, whilst an increasingly visible number of Muslim activists in Britain are hell bent on mass conversions to their brand of hard-line Islam. To block this phenomenon from scrutiny for fear of insult or consequence is to lose the battle of ideas before we even begin.

2. Anti-Semitism is based on outright fabrications that have haunted Europe for centuries: the historical spectre of blood libel, the Protocols of the Elders of Zion, the lie of Jewish conspiracies. However, a phobia of Islam is based on real acts of violence that have been committed and justified in the name of the religion in opposition to the moderate Islam practiced by hundreds of millions around the globe. In 2015, nearly three-quarters of terrorist attacks were perpetrated by the global Islamist movements Isis, Al-Qaeda, Boko Haram, and the Taliban. 7/7, Charlie Hebdo, the Manchester Arena bombing, and the Westminster bridge incident have brought these acts directly into British society, leading to an increased fear of the religion that is used to justify such violence.

3. The Jewish people are the last surviving civilisation from antiquity. All other Biblical communities – such as the Phoenicians, Hittites, Babylonians – are no more. Throughout history, this exceptional people has suffered violence and attempts at annihilation at the hands of the Egyptian pharaohs, Persians, Romans, fourteenth-century Iberian princes, the Russian tsars, and more recently by Hitler and Stalin. How can Muslims, a proud and over two-billion-strong global community, with a long history of empire and conquest, seek the same

protections as a tiny group of long-suffering people who are still reeling from the loss of millions of their people across Europe?

Conclusion: Politicians and Civil Society

Politics and politicians provide the tone, tenor, and tenets of modern civil society. The ancients used to say, 'the fish rots from the head down'. However flawed, in a democracy, leadership comes from Parliament. To surrender to the grievances and victimhood collectivism of Muslim activists is to do a disservice to Britain, liberty, and ordinary Muslims. As a Muslim, I would be branded an 'Islamophobe' and prosecuted, possibly jailed, for questioning interpretations of the Quran that continue to discriminate against women regarding violence, divorce, custody or inheritance.

If we in mainstream western society, in the press, in universities, cannot criticise the interpretations of Islam that lead to intolerance, sexism, racism, and violence, then we will empower and embolden large sections of the far right. This is already underway with the growth of the AfD in Germany, the National Front in France, the Party for Freedom in Holland, Fidesz in Hungary, and the prominence of figures like Tommy Robinson here in the UK.

The criminalisation of open discussion will undo the freedoms on which we all thrive.

British democracy must not succumb to the identity politics of contemporary hard-line Islamists who seek to subvert the West. We cannot rest on our laurels; we must be ever alert to threats to our hard-won liberties. Athenian democracy, subverted by an organised mob, sentenced Socrates to death in 399 BC because he questioned and mocked the gods of ancient Greece. In the spirit of Socrates, Moses, Jesus, and

Mohammed, we must continue to question all that is sacred and let our God-given 'natural light of reason' guide us to a world of human dignity despite our differences. As Immanuel Kant wrote in 1784, 'For enlightenment of this kind, all that is needed is freedom. And the freedom in question is the most innocuous form of all – freedom to make public use of one's reason in all matters.'

Maryam Namazie

The All-Party Parliamentary Group (APPG) on British Muslims' definition of Islamophobia has mainly been framed as a free speech issue. The definition adopted by some parties and councils will certainly limit criticism of Islam and Islamism even further than it already is currently. To say it will not is dishonest at best. This has already been the case for a long time now. For those of us who have fled Iran, it has been so since the expropriation of the Iranian revolution by the Islamists; in Britain, at least since the Rushdie affair.

Examples abound. The Council of Ex-Muslims of Britain, of which I am a Spokesperson, was placed under investigation for eight months by Pride in London because of the accusation of Islamophobia[1] levelled against us by the East London Mosque[2] and Mend.[3] I myself have been barred from Warwick University,[4] harassed by Islamic

---

[1] 'Muslim leaders make formal complaint over 'Islamophobic' banners at London Pride', Evening Standard, 14 July 2017, available at: https://www.standard.co.uk/news/london/muslim-leaders-make-formal-complaint-after-islamophobic-banners-spotted-at-london-pride-a3587351.html

[2] 'London school girl who recruited three classmates to join IS in Syria was 'radicalised at East London Mosque', Evening Standard, 2 August 2015, available at: https://www.standard.co.uk/news/london/london-schoolgirl-who-recruited-three-classmates-to-join-is-in-syria-was-radicalised-at-east-london-10433150.html

[3] 'Muslim lobby group Muslim Engagement and Development 'promotes extremism'', The Times, 31 October 2017, available at: https://www.thetimes.co.uk/article/muslim-lobby-group-promotes-extremism-muslim-engagement-and-development-mend-hkm87fx35

[4] 'Student union blocks speech by 'inflammatory' anti-sharia activist', Guardian, 26 September 2015, available at: https://www.theguardian.com/education/2015/sep/26/student-union-blocks-speech-activist-maryam-namazie-warwick

Society students at Goldsmiths,[5] and had my talk cancelled at Trinity College over the same accusations.[6] I haven't had issues for a while now – but that is only because I am hardly invited to speak at universities anymore. It is just too much trouble. The accusations stick; uncomfortably so.

Whilst this is a free speech issue (blasphemy is clearly not racism), what I find even more disturbing about this definition is the Parliamentary Group's open promulgation of the idea that there is something that can be called 'expressions of Muslimness.' It is absurd to assume that this is the case, any more than one can speak of expressions of Christianness or Jewishness or Hinduness. This is no different from saying there are 'expressions of Britishness'; something that the far-Right – and increasingly, mainstream politicians – imply in order to exclude migrants and minorities.

Certainly, we can discuss what it means to be British – or Muslim for that matter. This will inevitably mean different things to different people. But with the Brexit Party, Nigel Farage, Boris Johnson, Tommy Robinson, the Windrush scandal, May's 'Go Home' vans, and her 'hostile environment', along with the far-Right fascist parties gaining seats across Europe, the promotion of expressions of 'Britishness' isn't as innocent as it is made out to be. In this context, Britishness becomes *whiteness*. Likewise, promoting 'Muslimness' in a world in which the religious-Right is in power and causing havoc is far more ominous than it might initially seem.

---

[5] 'Muslim students from Goldsmiths University's Islamic Society 'heckle and aggressively interrupt' Maryam Namazie talk', 4 December 2015, available at: https://www.independent.co.uk/student/news/muslim-students-from-goldsmiths-university-s-islamic-society-heckle-and-aggressively-interrupt-a6760306.html

[6] 'Activist claims Trinity speech on apostasy and Islam cancelled', Irish Times, 22 March 2015, available at: https://www.irishtimes.com/news/politics/activist-claims-trinity-speech-on-apostasy-and-islam-cancelled-1.2149050

Like 'Britishness', the concept of 'Muslimness' is fundamentally about exclusion. Britishness tends to exclude brown and black people. Muslimness tends to exclude doubters and dissenters – anyone not 'authentically' regressive enough, not veiled enough, not segregated enough, not submissive enough, not pro-Sharia enough, not modest enough, not angry enough and not offended enough. Everyone else is an 'Islamophobe', an 'Uncle Tom', a 'native informant', a 'coconut' or a 'westernised, neo-colonialist.'

The not-so-funny thing about identity politics is that whilst it claims that each particular 'group' has a singular identity (as if that were even possible), the identity is so restrictive that it keeps out many more people than it allows in. In fact, that's the whole point. If you want in, you have to make sure you look the part and follow the rules. If you terrorise a primary school in Birmingham to prevent lessons saying that being gay is OK, if you defend Sharia courts despite their promotion of violence against women, or legitimise apostates being shunned and killed, then you will automatically pass the Muslimness authenticity test! Not so much if you are a gay Muslim, or an ex-Muslim, or a feminist who doesn't want to wear the hijab or fast during Ramadan, or a secularist who is opposed to Sharia law.

Another major problem with identity politics is that those with power determine Britishness or Muslimness or Jewishness or Hinduness and the limits of permissibility within these 'groups'. Therefore, 'Muslimness' becomes what Cage, Mend, the Muslim Council of Britain or the Iranian and Saudi regimes say it is. In Trump's US, Christianness passes regressive anti-abortion laws and moves to end Roe V Wade. In Modi's India, Hinduness means that one can be murdered for eating beef.

The Parliamentary Group's promotion of identity politics

and 'Muslimness,' has, therefore, everything to do with appeasing the religious-Right by pushing the false narrative of an 'authentic' Muslim: a homogenised caricature imposed upon a diverse people by fundamentalists-playing-victims.

This feeds into stereotypes, and collaborates in the erasure of class politics, dissent and political and social struggles; it diminishes solidarity both within and without the so-called group. Also, ironically, it actually exacerbates racism by insisting that brown and black citizens are 'different' and in need of paternalistic protection and treated with hyper-sensitivity in case (god forbid) they start burning books... or worse.

The politics of difference (and superiority) have always been a pillar of fascist and racist politics whether that difference is based on race or – as we now increasingly see – 'culture.' (Whose culture this is does not get discussed. Is it the culture of the Islamists who want to stone people to death or the women and men who refuse and resist?) For me, it is clear as daylight: the adoption of any definition of 'Islamophobia' is a triumph for fundamentalists. It has nothing to do with combatting racism.

A few other key points:

- Religion and belief are personal matters; lived experiences as varied as the people who hold them. Homogenising countless diverse people based on essentialised characteristics is part of a fundamentalist project designed to manage dissent. It has everything to do with power and control, and nothing to do with the right to freedom of belief and religion, or the fight against racism.

- Equalities legislation already considers discrimination against someone on the basis of protected characteristics such as religion or belief against the law. The insistence on normalising the term 'Islamophobia' appeases fundamentalists by conflating criticism of Islam and Islamism with bigotry against Muslims in order to restrict free expression, particularly blasphemy and heresy.

- Free speech matters most to minorities and migrants, the poor, disenfranchised, witches, apostates and heretics. Popes and imams, capitalists and kings don't need it; they already have access to all the forms of expression available, as well as the brute violence to back it up. Any limit on free speech limits the rights of the oppressed and aids the oppressor – even if the oppressor belongs to a 'minority' religion.

- Free speech is an individual right. It is not a group right. It is I who decides how to exercise my free speech, not the APPG nor any 'useful tests' proposed by some professor such as Tariq Modood to ascertain if my speech is to be considered 'reasonable criticism' or 'Islamophobic.' With limits, speech is no longer free.

- Finally, as needs to be clarified in any discussion of Islamophobia: rejecting the term 'Islamophobia' itself, or rejecting any attempts at defining it, does not mean that anti-Muslim bigotry doesn't exist. The rise in hate crimes and xenophobia, the dehumanisation of those deemed 'other', the criminalisation of migration and those helping desperate migrants all make the continued fight against racism as urgent as ever. Racism is a matter of life and death at worst and humiliation and discrimination at best for many people from Muslim, minority and refugee backgrounds. But fighting racism by imposing blasphemy laws gives the impression that something is being done against racism. Racism, however, is only being exacerbated by promoting difference and superiority, rather than secularism, citizenship, equality and our common humanity irrespective of background and belief.

Mohammed Amin MBE

Modern usage of 'Islamophobia' comes from the 1997 report by the Commission on British Muslims and Islamophobia: *Islamophobia: A Challenge for Us All*.[1]

I wrote in 2012 that the report was seriously flawed, because it conflates attitudes towards Islam and attitudes towards Muslims.[2] Re-reading the report while composing this article I noted that it does not contain a short, quotable definition of *'Islamophobia'*; perhaps one of the many disadvantages of committee authorship.

Subsequently, there have been attempts to steer the word Islamophobia away from its somewhat nebulous Runnymede 2017 definition, and instead to use it as a shorthand for reprehensible behaviours such as:

- anti-Muslim hatred,

- anti-Muslim bigotry,

- anti-Muslim prejudice,

- anti-Muslim discrimination.[3]

---

[1] 'Islamophobia: A Challenge for Us All', *Runnymede Trust*, 1997, available at: https://www.runnymedetrust.org/companies/17/74/Islamophobia-A-Challenge-for-Us-All.html

[2] Mohammed Amin, 'Islamophobia: A Trap for Unwary Muslims', Published on *MohammedAmin.com*, 26 July 2012, available at: https://www.mohammedamin.com/Community_issues/Islamophobia-a-trap-for-unwary-Muslims.html

[3] Farah Elahi and Omar Khan (ed), 'Islamophobia Still a challenge for us all', *Runnymede Trust*, 2018, available at: https://www.runnymedetrust.org/uploads/Islamophobia%20Report%202018%20FINAL.pdf

However, when people seek to use *'Islamophobia'* as a shorthand for the above behaviours, others respond by asserting their freedom to have negative views of Islam, and profess a legitimate fear of Islam, thereby harking back to the original meaning of 'Islamophobia' as understood by the Runnymede 2017 report.

Subsequent attempts to rescue the word 'Islamophobia' with a new definition

Given the widespread criticism of the 1997 Runnymede definition, there have been several attempts to rescue 'Islamophobia' with a revised definition.

- In 2017, to mark the 20th anniversary of the 1997 report, Runnymede published *Islamophobia: Still a challenge for us all.*[4]

- In June 2018, the organisation Muslim Engagement & Development (MEND) published their report *More than words: Approaching a definition of Islamophobia.*[5]

- In November 2018, the APPG on British Muslims issued its report: *Islamophobia Defined: The inquiry into a working definition of Islamophobia.*[6]

Some of the definitions are too long to reproduce here. I recommend instead glancing at the full reports linked above. These attempts to rescue the word are doomed to fail for two reasons.

---

[4] Ibid.
[5] 'More Than Words: Approaching a Definition of Islamophobia', MEND, June 2018, available at: https://mend.org.uk/wp-content/uploads/2018/06/Approaching-a-definition-of-Islamophobia-More-than-words.pdf
[6] Islamophobia Defined, All-Party Parliamentary Group on British Muslims, available at: https://static1.squarespace.com/static/599c3d2febbd1a90cffdd8a9/t/5bfd1ea3352f531a6170ceee/1543315109493/Islamophobia+Defined.pdf

1. A definition cannot be enforced by the Government

In France, the Académie Française guards the French language. It fights a noble, but largely unsuccessful, campaign to defend the French language from incursions by foreign words. English is quite different. There is no overarching authority. Words in English mean whatever the generality of English users decide that they mean.

The Government can legislate definitions for statutory purposes. As a tax adviser, I spent years advising clients about the definition of *'loan relationship'* for tax purposes, originally contained in the Finance Act 1996. However, such statutory definitions apply only for the purposes specified. That Act could not, and did not seek to, alter the meaning of the words *'loan relationship'* as used by citizens in their daily lives. (I have yet to meet a citizen who uses the words *'loan relationship'* for any purpose other than taxation.)

Accordingly, the Government could, if so minded, legislate a definition of *'Islamophobia'* for use by the criminal justice system. The definition would need to be tightly drawn so that it could be unambiguously applied by the courts. I suspect the Government regards that task as superfluous. We already have laws covering:

• racially motivated hate crime,

• religiously motivated hate crime,

• incitement to racial hatred,

• incitement to religious hatred,

• discrimination because of a person's race,

• discrimination because of a person's religion or belief.

Each of the above is defined in law without any need for a statutory definition of the word *'Islamophobia.'* Accordingly,

I fail to see how creating a statutory definition would help the legal system.

In theory, the existence of a definition for statutory purposes might change the way that the word 'Islamophobia' is understood by the man in the street. However, as most people have little interaction with statute law, I am dubious.

2. The long dissemination of the old definition makes it hard for any new definition to replace it

For 20 years, proponents of the word 'Islamophobia' attempted to defend the Runnymede 1997 definition.

Trying to use 'Islamophobia' as a synonym for the anti-Muslim bad behaviours enumerated above, while also adhering to the Runnymede 1997 definition, ran into a brick wall of opposition. Namely the Runnymede 1997 definition is about much more than those anti-Muslim bad behaviours. It is about an attitude towards Islam.

The Runnymede 1997 definition was appalling and has led to 'Islamophobia' becoming a 'crock of a word', as Douglas Murray described it in the *Jewish Chronicle* in 2013.[7]

Subsequent attempts to repair the 1997 damage with reports such as Runnymede 2017 have suffered from two flaws:

1. Unwillingness to explicitly abandon the Runnymede 1997 definition.

2. Use of the word 'racism', a word which means something entirely different to sociology academics and to the man in the street. The man in the street knows that Muslims are not a race, so how can you be racist against Muslims?

---

[7] Douglas Murray, 'We must stop avoiding this discussion', *Jewish Chronicle*, 24 June 2013, available at:
https://www.thejc.com/comment/comment/we-must-stop-avoiding-this-discussion-1.46179

It is time to abandon the word 'Islamophobia' because using it harms Muslims

It diverts attention from serious anti-Muslim bad behaviours, as enumerated above, and instead draws people into a wholly unproductive debate about the meaning of the word *'Islamophobia.'* Every minute spent in such a debate is a minute when we are not talking about anti-Muslim hatred.

If people desperately want a single word to be a strict Muslim analogue to antisemitism, then a new word must be invented. It needs to be a new word, to escape the baggage which the proponents of the word 'Islamophobia' have allowed to build up around it.

I have elsewhere proposed the word 'antimuslimism' (in my article 'Defining and promoting the word 'antimuslimism'')[8] and offered a definition modelled very closely on the IHRA definition of antisemitism.

In November 2018, the APPG issued its report *Islamophobia Defined: The inquiry into a working definition of Islamophobia*. The 72-page report covers the history of previous definitions of Islamophobia and many other related topics. Before issuing its report, the APPG received a great deal of evidence from academics and representatives of civil society organisations.

As with Runnymede 2017, the above definition uses the word 'racism' the way that sociologists do. Accordingly, it inevitably leads to the same arguments in response, namely that 'Muslims are not a race, so how can you be racist against them?'

Accordingly, I consider that the APPG's definition is simply not useful to Muslims or to anyone else.

---

[8] Mohammed Amin, 'Defining and promoting the word 'antimuslimism'', Published on *MohammedAmin.com*, 4 February 2019, available at: https://www. mohammedamin.com/Community_issues/Defining-antimuslimism.html

Open letters against adoption of the APPG's definition

I have signed two open letters to the Government advising against adopting the APPG's definition

1. Letter organised by National Secular Society (NSS) and published on 9 December 2018

The three key paragraphs reproduced below explain why the NSS was concerned:

> The report's core point is that the Government should make it policy to define Islamophobia as 'a type of racism that targets expressions of Muslimness or perceived Muslimness'. However, 'expressions of Muslimness' can effectively be translated to mean Islamic practices. In a society which is free and open, such practices must remain open to scrutiny and debate.

> Further, the report's backers are keen to stress the need to avoid shutting down criticism of religion. However, advancing the report's ill-defined concept of 'Islamophobia' and aligning it with the five 'tests' it recommends to determine whether speech is 'Islamophobic', will clearly render legitimate commentary and debate about Islam beyond the bounds of reasonable public debate.

> Far from combatting prejudice and bigotry, erroneous claims of 'Islamophobia' have become a cover for it. LGBT rights campaigners have been called 'Islamophobes' for criticising the views of Muslim clerics on homosexuality. Meanwhile, ex-Muslims and feminist activists have been called 'Islamophobes' for criticising certain Islamic views and practices relating to women. Even liberal and secular Muslims have been branded 'Islamophobes'.

2. Letter organised by Civitas and published on 15 May 2019

The letter explains in two pages what is wrong with the APPG's definition. Three key paragraphs are reproduced below:

> We are concerned that the definition will be used to shut down legitimate criticism and investigation. While the APPG authors have assured that it does not wish to infringe free speech, the entire content of the report, the definition itself, and early signs of how it would be used, suggest that it certainly would. Civil liberties should not be treated as an afterthought in the effort to tackle antiMuslim prejudice.

> The conflation of race and religion employed under the confused concept of 'cultural racism' expands the definition beyond anti-Muslim hatred to include 'illegitimate' criticism of the Islamic religion. The concept of Muslimness can effectively be transferred to Muslim practices and beliefs, allowing the report to claim that criticism of Islam is instrumentalised to hurt Muslims.

> No religion should be given special protection against criticism. Like anti-Sikh, anti-Christian, or anti-Hindu hatred, we believe the term anti-Muslim hatred is more appropriate and less likely to infringe on free speech. A proliferation of 'phobias' is not desirable, as already stated by Sikh and Christian organisations who recognise the importance of free discussion about their beliefs.

National Secular Society

The gatekeepers of public debate can't patronise away anti-Muslim bigotry

It's reasonable to assume good intentions lay behind the all-party parliamentary group on British Muslims' decision to issue a report outlining a proposed definition of 'Islamophobia' in November 2018.

On 15 March this year an Australian man walked into the Al Noor Mosque in Christchurch in New Zealand and shot people indiscriminately for around five minutes. He then drove to another mosque around three miles away and opened fire again.

By the time he was finished 49 people had died. In the subsequent weeks, two more would die from their injuries. If a worshipper had not managed to disarm the gunman, or the police had not been able to disarm his improvised explosive devices, the carnage would have been even more severe.

The Christchurch terrorist attack may have happened on the other side of the world, but it did not happen in a vacuum. And something similar could very possibly happen here in the UK.

In the weeks before the APPG's report came out, a car driver, apparently egged on by three passengers, drove into a number of pedestrians outside a mosque in north London.[1]

---

[1] Danny Boyle, 'Cricklewood mosque 'hate crime' crash: Three hurt as car hits crowd after 'tirade of racist abuse'', *The Telegraph*, 19th September 2018 https://www.telegraph.co.uk/news/2018/09/19/cricklewood-mosque-hate-crime-crash-three-hurt-car-swerves-crowd/

Police said the vehicle hit 'a number of pedestrians' and it was 'extremely fortunate' nobody had died. Three people were injured.

A man from Lincoln also admitted sending hundreds of letters around the country threatening Muslims during a sustained two-year campaign.[2] These included threats of a 'Punish a Muslim day', with 'rewards' offered for attacks on people and mosques.

Some of his letters contained white powder as a hoax poison. One letter to Muslim worshippers in Hull said they would be 'slaughtered very soon'. Another, to the University of Sheffield, said he would donate money to charity every time a Muslim was killed.

And these were just the most high-profile anti-Muslim crimes to take place in that time.

These were attacks on Muslims' religious freedom. They demanded the full force of the law being brought to bear against the perpetrators. And they should prompt society to seek to challenge the attitudes behind them.

So it was not surprising that the APPG's report included examples of anti-Muslim hate crimes which should be universally condemned: a mother attacked for wearing a hijab as she went to pick her children up from school; racists leaving pig's heads or bacon strips at mosque entrances; a man trying to kill a Muslim woman and girl. The report also drew on the wider problem of anti-Muslim discrimination.

The report identified a genuine problem. But the solution it suggested would worsen the problem – and do so while restricting public discussion.

The report used the word 'Islamophobia', overriding the objections of the National Secular Society (NSS) and

---

[2] 'Lincoln man admits sending 'Punish a Muslim Day' letters', *BBC News*, 12th October 2018 https://www.bbc.co.uk/news/uk-england-45838506

groups such as Southall Black Sisters, which campaigns for the rights of women from minority groups. Unfortunately, the term has now been normalised in public debate. Major press outlets use it with impunity and politicians appear to feel little shame using it. This has undermined rather than boosted minority rights. (For a better exploration of this topic readers should consult a nuanced and well-reasoned blog post from Kenan Malik.)[3]

The authors' decision to use the term 'Islamophobia' was instructive of their wider approach. At the report's launch, Sayeeda (Baroness) Warsi, a prominent member of the APPG, expressed her reservations over the use of the term but said she was persuaded to go along with it, because the Muslim 'community' preferred it.

The report consistently sided with contributors who claimed to represent the 'community'. This may be a reflection of the influence of Warsi, who consistently claims to do the same, with minimal pushback in large chunks of the British press. Shortly before the report was published she claimed 'British Muslim communities' were 'fully supportive of any asylum claim Asia Bibi may have' in the House of Lords, referring to a woman being hunted by mobs over her alleged 'blasphemy' in Pakistan.[4] On what authority Warsi spoke for 3.4m people, nobody made clear.[5] It may also be a reflection of the thinking of Naz Shah, who

---

[3] Kenan Malik, 'Rethinking the Challenge of Anti-Muslim Bigotry', *KenanMalik. com*, Nov 2017 https://kenanmalik.com/2017/11/15/rethinking-the-challenge-of-anti-muslim-bigotry/

[4] House of Lords, 'Asia Bibi' Debate Vol. 794, 20 November 2018, available at: https://hansard.parliament.uk/Lords/2018-11-20/debates/EC780CC3-1DC2-44FD-B1BC-0384CD1377F3/AsiaBibi

[5] 'Muslim population in the UK', *Office for National Statistics*, 2 August 2018, available at: https://www.ons.gov.uk/aboutus/transparencyandgovernance/freedomofinformationfoi/muslimpopulationintheuk/

claimed to 'represent' the 'community' when the report was launched.

The APPG describes part of its mission as 'celebrating the contributions of Muslim communities in the UK'. And siding with the ill-defined 'community' meant dismissing concerns about free speech. The report regularly paid lip service to the need to avoid shutting down criticism of religion. But at no point did it engage with concerns that those who raise criticisms of Islamic practices and religious privileges which undermine women's rights, animal welfare, free speech, LGBT rights and the principle of one law for all are routinely shouted down as Islamophobes or Islamophobe enablers.

At one point it said: 'The right to free speech ends when words and actions begin to 'fuel hatred, violence and stimulate antagonistic responses which are at odds with the cohesive society'. Upon this concept, we heard that a definition of Islamophobia could perhaps be cognizant of the legal elements of 'intent' and 'recklessness' when determining the boundaries for policing free speech.'

And the authors proposed vague and unworkable plans which would do exactly what they said they would not do.

The report said the government should make it policy that 'Islamophobia is rooted in racism and is a type of racism that targets expressions of Muslimness or perceived Muslimness'. 'Expressions of Muslimness' can roughly be translated to mean Islamic practices. Why else would the launch have heard that any definition of 'Islamophobia' must include instances of Ofsted inspectors questioning the wearing of the hijab by young girls in primary schools?

The report also gives a – non-exhaustive – series of examples of speech that could be officially declared 'Islamophobic'. Claiming that 'Muslim identity' has 'a unique propensity for terrorism' would be a 'myth' which would apparently need to be shut down. Pointing out the link between Islam and terrorism is likely to become even less acceptable than it already is.

It also declared accusations that Muslims or Muslim majority states 'invent or exaggerate Islamophobia', or accusations that Muslims are more loyal to the priorities of Muslims worldwide than their own countries, beyond the pale. Bigots may make these points for their own ends, but reasonable people may also ask how far there is some truth in them. And did the authors not think we should point out that Muslim theocracies push propaganda in an attempt to convince Muslims that British society hates them?

The APPG also approvingly cited five 'tests' to determine whether speech is 'Islamophobic':

- Does it stereotype Muslims by assuming they all think the same?

- Is it about Muslims or a dialogue with Muslims, which they would wish to join in?

- Is mutual learning possible?

- Is the language civil and contextually appropriate?

- Does the person doing the criticism really care about the issue or [are they] using it to attack Muslims?

There may be newspaper columns, reports from think tanks or comments made towards Muslims in the street which deserve criticism on some of these grounds. But as tests which could render some commentary beyond the bounds of public debate they were utterly unworkable. That is particularly so as the APPG suggested that if the answer to any of these questions is 'yes', the comment may constitute 'Islamophobia'.

Warsi herself seemed to imply that all Muslims think the same in the comments in the Lords mentioned above. Muslim exceptionalists regularly suggest Muslims cannot possibly cope with other people being allowed to draw Muhammad or that Muslims cannot possibly eat meat from animals which have been stunned before slaughter. Do they get away with it because they are seen to be on the Muslim 'side'?

Why should non-Muslims not discuss Muslims? Is there any other group of people who do not get or should not get talked about? What 'mutual learning' are we expected to do when the Islamic practice or attitude in question is wrong and the person criticising it is right? Does the call for 'civil' language mean blunt criticism is phobic?

How on earth can we read the mind of someone who says something critical to know whether they 'really care about the issue'? Should we dismiss any criticism of non-stun slaughter that does not come from a vegetarian? On what grounds will those who advocate Muslim integration be allowed to speak at all?

And most importantly who will monitor the debate, deciding what is acceptable and what is not? At the report's launch Liam Byrne MP called for changes in the law and court action against media outlets for 'hate speech'. In a parliamentary debate in May he reiterated the point by saying the definition would be used to 'prosecute Islamophobia and to clamp down on its enablers in the British media'.

The report regularly attacked the press and uncritically mentioned that 'community' representatives have called for 'accountability for media'. Hidden within the report was a power grab.

And that power grab could reach into every area of British life, as the report repeatedly refers to the apparent problem of 'institutional Islamophobia'. This relativistic idea suggests the need for a wholesale change in British society to accommodate Muslims and lets Muslim culture off the hook for problems Muslims face.

Would an employer, for example, be characterised as a '-phobe' for refusing to promote or hire people who push their religion on their colleagues, or whose religion interferes with the quality of their work? It is already against the law to discriminate against people on the basis of their faith, for example in employment. So what else would need to change before we can stop calling British society 'institutionally Islamophobic'?

All-party parliamentary groups do not have any power to change the law or government policy. But this report has been uncritically embraced in much of Westminster and by some local authorities and public bodies. The government has rightly rejected it, but it still seems set to have a significant influence on the rough parameters of acceptable public debate on Islam for years to come.

The government could do many things to address bigotry against Muslims and other religious groups. It could tackle the division of British schools along faith lines. It could face up to religious separatism and start enforcing the same laws for everyone, regardless of religion. That might also make an impact on intra-religious sectarianism (an issue which the APPG's report deliberately ducks). But these things are difficult and have a less obvious, gradual impact. It's easier to try to tell people what they may or may not say.

It's now routine for those in positions of power to try to patronise bigotry away. Last year the NSS took up the case of Justice Haddon-Cave – a judge who lectured the Parsons Green bomber on the peacefulness of Islam and encouraged him to study the Koran in prison.[6] The authorities responded to this blatant violation of judicial neutrality with a collective shrug of the shoulders.[7]

Haddon-Cave's comments were ignored on the grounds that the British public must be lectured by their apparent betters on how wonderful Islam is. And he was allowed to repeat his remarks almost verbatim as he wrapped up the trial of a man convicted of attempting to kill the prime minister.[8]

Meanwhile it's becoming increasingly difficult to get on a train, turn on the TV or go to a bookshop without being patronised on Islam. A recent poster campaign has told members of the public 'it's not just offensive – it's an offence', reinforcing the message that the British public cannot be trusted to treat their fellow citizens who happen to have a different religion with respect.

Islamic terrorism only played a minor part in the recent series *Bodyguard*. Without wishing to ruin it for anyone who hasn't yet seen it, this six-part series which was entirely about terrorism and security largely steered clear of Islam and Muslims. At one point there was an attempt to frame a brown-skinned man for a terrorist act; this was presented

---

[6] 'NSS: judge shouldn't have interpreted Islam when sentencing bomber', *National Secular Society*, 27 March 2018, available at: https://www.secularism.org.uk/news/2018/03/nss-judge-shouldnt-have-interpreted-islam-when-sentencing-bomber

[7] 'NSS appeals to ombudsman over judge's remarks on Islam', National Secular Society, 27 June 2018, available at: https://www.secularism.org.uk/news/2018/06/nss-appeals-to-ombudsman-over-judges-remarks-on-islam; 'Theology isn't secular courts' business, NSS tells justice secretary', *National Secular Society*, 28 September 2018, available at: https://www.secularism.org.uk/news/2018/09/theology-isnt-secular-courts-business-nss-tells-justice-secretary

[8] 'REGINA v Naa'imur Zakariyah RAHMAN, Sentencing Remarks of the Hon. Mr Justice Haddon-Cave', *Judiciary of England and Wales*, available at: https://www.judiciary.uk/wp-content/uploads/2018/09/r-v-rahman-sentencing.doc.pdf

unsympathetically as an unscrupulous tactic to play on anti-Muslim prejudice. But inevitably the show has still been criticised – including, unsurprisingly, from Warsi – on the basis that one character represented a 'stereotypical' view of Muslim women.[9]

And in the same week the APPG's report was published, it was reported that a novel about a suicide bomber who changes his mind after going to a library had been pulled from publication amid mob outrage and cries of 'Islamophobia'. When *The Guardian* reported that story, it did not feature a single comment from anyone defending the right to publish the book.[10] Did it occur to those writing and editing the story that this might be unreasonable censorship, restricting people's right to read the novel?

These silencing tactics do not work. The best approach to the thorny issues created by multiculturalism isn't to shut down debate; it is to change our whole approach and embrace free speech, with all its imperfections.

And that applies beyond the subject of Islam. There are significant differences between the proposed Islamophobia definition and the much-discussed International Holocaust Remembrance Alliance's definition of anti-Semitism. Most importantly, the IHRA describes anti-Semitism as 'a certain perception of Jews' – a group of people – whereas the APPG's phrase 'expressions of Muslimness' affords protection to religious practices and beliefs.

---

[9] Deborah Orr, 'Baroness Warsi: BBC's Bodyguard stereotyped Muslim women — either they're downtrodden or a terrorist', *Radio Times*, 15 November 2018, available at: https://www.radiotimes.com/news/radio/2018-11-15/baroness-warsi-bodyguard-stereotyped-muslim-women/

[10] Alison Flood, 'Graphic novel 'steeped in Islamophobia' pulled after protests', *Guardian*, 26 November 2018, available at: https://www.theguardian.com/books/2018/nov/26/a-suicide-bomber-sits-in-the-library-comic-pulled-protests-jack-gantos-dave-mckean

But there are also similarities. Reading through the report it is clear that its authors have learnt from recent debates on anti-Semitism. For instance, according to one of its examples it would be 'Islamophobic' to claim that the existence of 'an independent Palestine or Kashmir is a terrorist endeavour'. That has echoes of the furore over describing Israel's founding as inherently racist.

In the case of bigotry against both Jews and Muslims bigots will hide behind the right to criticise ideologies, but official policy should err on the side of free speech. It is for civil society to expose intellectual dishonesty, defeat it and marginalise it.

The authors also cite existing restrictions on speech under counter-terrorism or counter-extremism legislation – for example, restrictions on speech which 'glorifies' terrorism – as a justification for restricting speech critical of Islam or Muslims. As the NSS has argued as part of the Defend Free Speech campaign, it's misguided to push vague official definitions in an attempt to make a problem go away.[11]

We all have an interest in people's right to go about their daily business without being harassed or abused. We also all have an interest in the mutual right to speak freely and to be given the benefit of the doubt until we comprehensively show we do not deserve it.

The members of the APPG on British Muslims are just the latest to suggest these two aims are in opposition. But censorship creates resentment. Resentment generates bigotry. Ending censorship is one of a series of steps we can take to push bigots back to the fringes of society. If we want social harmony, we should put a bit of trust in our fellow citizens to speak and think freely.

---

[11] 'Defend free speech', *National Secular Society*, available at: https://www.secularism.org.uk/defend-free-speech/

David Toube

There is an old joke about a city dweller, lost in the countryside, looking for a nearby town. He approaches a yokel who is leaning on a gate and asks for directions. 'Well', he answers, 'If I were you, I wouldn't start from here'.

We badly need a functioning definition of Islamophobia: a yardstick which helps society draw the line. The fundamental problem with the APPG's proposed definition is that it starts from the wrong place. As a result, it fails to reach its proper destination. It is not fit for purpose.

The starting point for the APPG definition, both in terms of structure and content, is the International Holocaust Remembrance Alliance (IHRA) working definition of Antisemitism. That was a mistaken choice. Antisemitism is, at its heart, a conspiracy theory about supernatural Jewish power, that imagines that Jews control politics, the media, and the financial system. It seeks to explain the world in these terms. Islamophobia, by contrast, operates in a rather different way. It makes a series of claims about Muslims: that the 'real Muslim' is a religiously-directed child rapist or terrorist: a medieval throwback who has no place in Western society.

Not all forms of hatred are identical. Bigotry draws upon deeply culturally rooted mythologies, which vary, depending upon the groups which they target. The Procrustean exercise, by which Islamophobia has been crammed into a structure designed to capture the essence of antisemitism, has seriously skewed the resultant definition.

Take, for example, the attempt to transpose the following part of the IHRA definition:

> Denying the Jewish people their right to self-determination, e.g., by claiming that the existence of a State of Israel is a racist endeavor.

It is commonplace for Jew-haters to argue that Israel should be destroyed and its population dispersed to those countries in which they experienced persecution. By contrast, those who hate Muslims may call for immigration bans and deportations: but they do not generally express their disdain by claiming that all Muslim states should be eradicated. Nevertheless, the APPG definition provides that Islamophobia includes:

> Denying Muslim populations the right to self-determination e.g., by claiming that the existence of an independent Palestine or Kashmir is a terrorist endeavour.

Since President Woodrow Wilson's 'Fourteen Points', self-determination of populations has been a foundational principle of international law. But it is not the case that the denial of any claim to self-determination is motivated by racism. Opposition to Scottish independence, for example, is not usually an expression of anti-Scottish racism.

Note also the shift from 'racist endeavour' to 'terrorist endeavour'. A Kashmir that was governed by Lashkar-e-Taiba would indeed be such a state. It is also clear that Gaza, under the rule of Hamas, would continue to devote its efforts to terrorist attacks with the goal of eliminating the whole of Israel, as promised by its founding Covenant. When ISIS declared its state, it was predictable that it would be a terrorist endeavour: and so it proved. If the purpose and effect of the formulation is to define as Islamophobia any expression of concerns such as these, it is objectionable. It is difficult to escape the conclusion that this outcome is precisely what the drafters of the APPG definition intended to achieve.

I mention this example not to express an opinion on the merits of an independent Kashmir or Palestine. There are reasonable arguments for both. Rather, it illustrates the mess which results from taking the wrong starting point.

Let's take another example. The IHRA definition provides that antisemitism includes:

> Accusing the Jews as a people, or Israel as a state, of inventing or exaggerating the Holocaust.

The APPG follow suit:

> Accusing Muslims as a group, or Muslim majority states, of inventing or exaggerating Islamophobia, ethnic cleansing or genocide perpetrated against Muslims.

There are certainly some specific incidents of politicians suggesting that particular cases of ethnic cleansing or genocide against Muslims are untrue. For example, in 2004, the Leader of the Opposition, Jeremy Corbyn sponsored an Early Day Motion that congratulated 'John Pilger on his expose of the fraudulent justifications for intervening in a 'genocide' that never really existed in Kosovo'. NATO's intervention in Kosovo was a successful attempt to prevent a genocide, akin to the one that had previously taken place in Srebrenica during the Bosnian war. Although it is shameful that Jeremy Corbyn signed that motion, his primary motivation was most likely a form of anti-Western anti-imperialism, rather than a generalised Islamophobia.

Again, the attempt to shoehorn Islamophobia into a model designed for antisemitism has deformed the concept.

Holocaust denial has an emblematic status. Antisemites routinely deny, play down, or engage in other forms of revisionism relating to the Holocaust. It is a type of conduct that is precisely calibrated to cause anguish to European Jews, most of whom experienced the murder of family members at the hands of Nazis, by suggesting that they are liars. But the denial of genocides is not a species of conduct that typifies Islamophobia.

There is an instructive departure from the IHRA definition in another part of the APPG text. The IHRA defines antisemitism as:

> Calling for, aiding, or justifying the killing or harming of Jews in the name of a radical ideology or an extremist view of religion.

By contrast, the APPG provides that Islamophobia includes:

> Calling for, aiding, instigating or justifying the killing or harming of Muslims in the name of a racist/ fascist ideology, or an extremist view of religion.

It is notable that the term 'radical' has been replaced by 'racist/fascist'. Why does the definition exclude radicals who are neither racists nor fascists? A possible explanation is that some of those who played a role in the drafting of the definition, themselves subscribe to a non-racist radical ideology which led them to cheer on various anti-Western regimes or Islamist theocrats which have harmed and killed many thousands of Muslims. Perhaps they fear that, were the term 'radical' employed in the definition, this support might be said to constitute Islamophobia. If that is the motivation, it is a pretty unimpressive one.

There are other important ways in which the APPG has started from the wrong place. The IHRA working definition drew on the work of academics with unblemished reputations and broadly accepted expertise, and was produced carefully, over a significant period of time. That was an important part of the process of crafting a definition which was capable of gaining widespread support and acceptance.

The same cannot be said of those who provided input to the APPG's efforts. Criticism has been made of the role played by an academic, Dr Antonio Perra, formerly of MEND. MEND is an organisation which promotes and defends radical preachers who have called for the establishment of a caliphate and supported military jihad to that end. Notably, a member of MEND's staff has been supportive of Hamas on social media. Perra himself has accused my organisation, Quilliam, of having borrowed 'elements of both Far-Right and Liberal Islamophobia'.

The APPG report also draws repeatedly on the work of a controversial academic, Professor David Miller of Bristol University, who is associated with a pro-Assad think tank. More to the point, Miller has expressed the view that Jewish students who fear antisemitism have been fooled by 'propaganda which they have been schooled with... there are organisations Israel lobby organisations Zionist movement organisations, some allied to the Israeli government...'. Indeed, Miller proudly breaches the IHRA definition on which the APPG's work is so closely based:

> [The creation of Israel] was by definition a racist endeavour, there's no getting away from that, I say that in cognizance that to say something that I've just said is regarded by lots of people as being antisemitic. It isn't.

It is, to put it politely, inappropriate that a definition of Islamophobia should draw on the work of such a person. If the object of the APPG exercise was to produce an untainted product, it has seriously failed.

There are other objections to the APPG definition. The chief substantive concern is that the definition is so loosely drafted that it will does not provide a helpful guide to conduct. This is, of course, a complaint that can be made about a proscriptive definition of any sort. However, it does not help that the APPG text rests upon a neologism: 'Muslimness', which is not generally used or understood, and is therefore open to multiple and conflicting interpretations. The function of a well-structured definition should be to provide as high a degree of certainty as possible. The APPG definition does not meet this test.

The indeterminacy of the definition has, in turn, caused further problems. By way of illustration, in the context of the dispute over teaching about the existence of gay people at Parkfield School, a campaigning Facebook page that supports the protestors claimed that the injunction obtained by Birmingham Council to prevent harassment of pupils and staff at the school breached the APPG definition. A well drafted text would not have raised such expectations.

Finally, I'd like to say a little bit about the use of the term 'Islamophobia', and its connection to what might be called 'intra-Muslim hatred'.

There are those who prefer the term: 'anti-Muslim bigotry'. I tend to use that formulation, because it is important to focus on the impact of hatred, discrimination, and violence that individuals suffer because of their identity. A reasonable criticism of the term 'Islamophobia' is that, in focusing on 'Islam' rather than 'Muslims' it may prohibit criticism of a belief system, in a manner akin to a blasphemy law.

It is important to recognise that there are forms of anti-Muslim hatred which amount to conspiracism about

Muslims and their beliefs. Take, for example, the suggestion that Muslims who appear to be politically and socially liberal are really 'stealth jihadists', who use 'taqiyya' to hide their true views. Taqiyya is a predominantly Shia theological concept which permits a limited degree of dissimulation about religious beliefs, in strictly defined circumstances, in the face of extreme persecution. There are certainly a number of takfiri and Islamist preachers who do believe that all Muslims have an religious and personal obligation to create and sustain a theocratic caliphate by means of military jihad. But it is obnoxious to insist that Muslims who reject such a political vision are lying. It should also be noted that the claim that Shia Muslims cannot be trusted to tell the truth about anything is routinely made by many Sunni Salafi preachers, who deploy the generalised accusation of taqiyyah in a very similar manner to non-Muslim bigots.

The characterisation of Islam as 'a single monolithic system, without internal development, diversity and dialogue' – as the Runnymede Trust's original 1997 definition put it – undeniably constitutes Islamophobia. If used in this manner, the term 'Islamophobia' is not one to which I object. It might also be argued that a takfirism which denies the richness and diversity of Islamic theology, jurisprudence and cultural practice is also a form of Islamophobia.

That observation leads to a related question: should the definition of Islamophobia include intra-Muslim prejudice? After all, the view that Ahmadis are not Muslims could be said to be a denial of the variety within Islam. Precisely this question was asked in the APPG's original consultation. For reasons which are not entirely clear, the APPG quietly removed it, a week before the deadline for responses.

Notwithstanding that takfirism, anti-Shia prejudice, and anti-Ahmadi incitement by some Sunni organisations have resulted in the horrific murders of Muslims, on balance, I think that they should not be regarded as forms of Islamophobia. They are best treated as the product of a different species of sectarianism: one which is perhaps more deadly to Muslims. But those examples illustrate the importance of a well crafted definition. It is arguable, on the face of the text, that intra-Muslim Islamophobia is caught by the APPG definition. That, in itself, is an illustration that the APPG has failed to draw the line in a manner which provides clarity and certainty.

Bigotry against Muslims isn't imagined. We have all encountered it. A well-crafted, broadly accepted definition will be a valuable tool. But this misguided search-and-replace exercise on the IHRA definition fails to hit the mark. Institutions, public organisations and politicians are now faced with an invidious choice: to implement a flawed definition which will inevitably be misapplied, or quietly to fail to endorse it.

But that is a false dichotomy. There is a third option. Don't start with the IHRA definition. Instead, go back to the drawing board, and use the actual experiences of Muslims who have faced snide remarks, discrimination and assaults to craft a functional definition, from the ground up.

We have one chance to get this right. If this opportunity is fluffed, another won't come along for many years.

Appendix

Open Letter: APPG Islamophobia Definition Threatens Civil Liberties

Addressed to the Home Secretary Sajid Javid

15 May 2019

The APPG on British Muslims' definition of Islamophobia has now been adopted by the Labour Party, the Liberal Democrats Federal board, Plaid Cymru and the Mayor of London, as well as several local councils. All of this is occurring before the Home Affairs Select Committee has been able to assess the evidence for and against the adoption of the definition nationally. Meanwhile the Conservatives are having their own debate about rooting out Islamophobia from the party.

According to the APPG definition, 'Islamophobia is rooted in racism and is a type of racism that targets expressions of Muslimness or perceived Muslimness'.

With this definition in hand, it is perhaps no surprise that following the horrific attack on a mosque in Christchurch, New Zealand, some place responsibility for the atrocity on the pens of journalists and academics who have criticised Islamic beliefs and practices, commented on or investigated Islamist extremism.

The undersigned unequivocally, unreservedly and emphatically condemn acts of violence against Muslims, and recognise the urgent need to deal with anti-Muslim hatred. However, we are extremely concerned about the uncritical and hasty adoption of the APPG's definition of Islamophobia.

This vague and expansive definition is being taken on without an adequate scrutiny or proper consideration of its negative consequences for freedom of expression, and academic and journalistic freedom. The definition will also undermine social cohesion – fuelling the very bigotry against Muslims which it is designed to prevent.

We are concerned that allegations of Islamophobia will be, indeed already are being, used to effectively shield Islamic beliefs and even extremists from criticism, and that formalising this definition will result in it being employed effectively as something of a backdoor blasphemy law.

The accusation of Islamophobia has already been used against those opposing religious and gender segregation in education, the hijab, halal slaughter on the grounds of animal welfare, LGBT rights campaigners opposing Muslim views on homosexuality, ex-Muslims and feminists opposing Islamic views and practices relating to women, as well as those concerned about the issue of grooming gangs. It has been used against journalists who investigate Islamism, Muslims working in counter-extremism, schools and Ofsted for resisting conservative religious pressure and enforcing gender equality.

Evidently abuse, harmful practices, or the activities of groups and individuals which promote ideas contrary to British values are far more likely to go unreported as a result of fear of being called Islamophobic. This will only increase if the APPG definition is formally adopted in law.

We are concerned that the definition will be used to shut down legitimate criticism and investigation. While the

APPG authors have assured that it does not wish to infringe free speech, the entire content of the report, the definition itself, and early signs of how it would be used, suggest that it certainly would. Civil liberties should not be treated as an afterthought in the effort to tackle anti-Muslim prejudice.

The conflation of race and religion employed under the confused concept of 'cultural racism' expands the definition beyond anti-Muslim hatred to include 'illegitimate' criticism of the Islamic religion. The concept of Muslimness can effectively be transferred to Muslim practices and beliefs, allowing the report to claim that criticism of Islam is instrumentalised to hurt Muslims.

No religion should be given special protection against criticism. Like anti-Sikh, anti-Christian, or anti-Hindu hatred, we believe the term anti-Muslim hatred is more appropriate and less likely to infringe on free speech. A proliferation of 'phobias' is not desirable, as already stated by Sikh and Christian organisations who recognise the importance of free discussion about their beliefs.

Current legislative provisions are sufficient, as the law already protects individuals against attacks and unlawful discrimination on the basis of their religion. Rather than helping, this definition is likely to create a climate of self-censorship whereby people are fearful of criticising Islam and Islamic beliefs. It will therefore effectively shut down open discussions about matters of public interest. It will only aggravate community tensions further and is therefore no long term solution.

If this definition is adopted the government will likely turn to self-appointed 'representatives of the community' to define 'Muslimness'. This is clearly open to abuse. The APPG already entirely overlooked Muslims who are often considered to be 'insufficiently Muslim' by other Muslims, moderates, liberals, reformers and the Ahmadiyyah, who often suffer persecution and violence at the hands of other Muslims.

For all these reasons, the APPG definition of Islamophobia is deeply problematic and unfit for purpose. Acceptance of this definition will only serve to aggravate community tensions and to inhibit free speech about matters of fundamental importance. We urge the government, political parties, local councils and other organisations to reject this flawed proposed definition.

Emma Webb, Civitas

Hardeep Singh, Network of Sikh Organisations (NSOUK)

Lord Singh of Wimbledon

Tim Dieppe, Christian Concern

Stephen Evans, National Secular Society (NSS)

Sadia Hameed, Council of Ex-Muslims of Britain (CEMB)

Prof. Paul Cliteur, candidate for the Dutch Senate, Professor of Law, University of Leiden

Brendan O'Neill, Editor of Spiked

Maajid Nawaz, Founder, Quilliam International

Rt. Rev'd Dr Gavin Ashenden

Pragna Patel, director of Southall Black Sisters

Professor Richard Dawkins

Rahila Gupta, author and journalist

Peter Whittle, founder and director of New Culture Forum

Trupti Patel, President of Hindu Forum of Britain

Dr Lakshmi Vyas, President Hindu Forum of Europe

Harsha Shukla MBE, President Hindu Council of North UK

Tarang Shelat, President Hindu Council of Birmingham

Ashvin Patel, Chairman, Hindu Forum (Walsall)

Ana Gonzalez, partner at Wilson Solicitors LLP

Baron Desai of Clement Danes

Baroness Cox of Queensbury

Lord Alton of Liverpool

Bishop Michael Nazir-Ali

Ade Omooma MBE, Co-Chair National Church Leaders Forum (NCLF)

Wilson Chowdhry, British Pakistani Christian Association

Ashish Joshi, Sikh Media Monitoring Group

Satish K Sharma, National Council of Hindu Temples

Rumy Hasan, academic and author

Amina Lone, Co-Director, Social Action and Research Foundation

Peter Tatchell, Peter Tatchell Foundation

Seyran Ateş, Imam

Gina Khan, One Law for All

Mohammed Amin MBE

Baroness D'Souza

Michael Mosbacher, Acting Editor, Standpoint Magazine

Lisa-Marie Taylor, CEO FiLiA

Julie Bindel, journalist and feminist campaigner

Dr Adrian Hilton, academic

Neil Anderson, academic

Tom Holland, historian

Toby Keynes

Prof. Dr. Bassam Tibi, Professor Emeritus for International Relations, University of Goettingen

Dr Stephen Law, philosopher and author

Maryam Namazie, Campaigner